The
ROPES

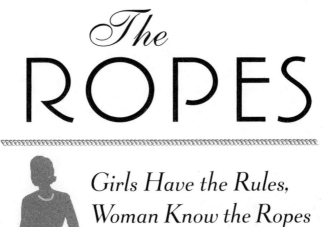

The
ROPES

Girls Have the Rules,
Woman Know the Ropes

JUDY STEINBERG and

RAECHEL DONAHUE

DUTTON

DUTTON
Published by Penguin Group (USA) Inc.
375 Hudson Street, New York, New York 10014, U.S.A.
Penguin Group (Canada), 10 Alcorn Avenue, Toronto, Ontario, Canada M4V 3B2 (a division of Pearson Penguin Canada Inc.); Penguin Books Ltd, 80 Strand, London WC2R 0RL, England; Penguin Ireland, 25 St Stephen's Green, Dublin 2, Ireland (a division of Penguin Books Ltd); Penguin Group (Australia), 250 Camberwell Road, Camberwell, Victoria 3124, Australia (a division of Pearson Australia Group Pty Ltd); Penguin Books India Pvt Ltd, 11 Community Centre, Panchsheel Park, New Delhi - 110 017, India; Penguin Group (NZ), cnr Airborne and Rosedale Roads, Albany, Auckland 1310, New Zealand (a division of Pearson New Zealand Ltd); Penguin Books (South Africa) (Pty) Ltd, 24 Sturdee Avenue, Rosebank, Johannesburg 2196, South Africa

Penguin Books Ltd, Registered Offices: 80 Strand, London WC2R 0RL, England

Published by Dutton, a member of Penguin Group (USA) Inc.

First printing, June 2005
10 9 8 7 6 5 4 3 2 1

LIBRARY OF CONGRESS CATALOGING-IN-PUBLICATION DATA

Steinberg, Judy.
    The ropes : girls have the rules, women know the ropes / by Judy Steinberg and Raechel Donahue.
        p. cm.
    Includes bibligraphical references and index.
    ISBN 0-525-94885-6 (alk. paper)
    1. Single women—Life skills guides.   2. Dating (Social customs)   3. Man-woman relationships.   I. Donahue, Raechel.   II. Title.

    HQ800.2.S74 2005
    306.7'082—dc22   2005001631

Printed in the United States of America
Set in Granjon
Designed by Helene Berinsky

To all women of every age
who believe in themselves.

CONTENTS

Contents

The
ROPES

Introduction

*E*ven as a young woman, I dreaded growing older with every year. I spent my thirtieth birthday (and every subsequent natal celebration that ended in a zero) alone in bed with the covers over my head and the drapes drawn. It's not that I'm shallow, but living the high life in Hollywood's celebrity society is a constant Iron Woman race against Time, with glamour nipping at your heels like a pit bull with a taste for Stuart Weitzman mules. Being pretty—or even beautiful— could never be good enough. One had to be on the cutting edge of fashion, have an encyclopedic knowledge of who was who, who was hot and, most importantly, who was on the way out.

It was stressful in a superficial sort of way, but I thrived on it because I had perfected being the celebrity wife. My clothes were outstanding yet not overstated; my dinners were well thought out and flawlessly executed, whether for two or twenty. Believe me, it's work to keep a dinner conversation going among twelve people who only want to talk about themselves.

I don't want to sound bitter, because we had some good times along the way, but there were other times I sat in the bathtub for hours, running more and more water, not to create more foam with the Giorgio bath gel, but trying to drown my unhappiness. I think the pain was sharpest when I realized that what I was feeling was loneliness.

And that was when I was still married to my husband, David Steinberg, before he dumped me for a fortyish casting agent who wrote a book called *How I Survived My Boyfriend's Divorce*. After that, my life became about surviving my husband's girlfriend's book and learning to live life on the skids of sidelined celebrity. I was dropped like a hot potato by all except a few old friends who were amazed that it lasted twenty-four years.

Then came the drama of entering the singles scene later in life. What a cruel awakening!

It was not the scene I had left behind at thirty. I felt like a fish out of water, flopping about and gasping for oxygen. It was not an experience for the faint of heart.

One bleak afternoon as I wallowed in the deep, dark abyss of menopause, I caught Cybill Shepherd on *The Oprah Winfrey Show* discussing her menopausal experience. She said something I found quite inspiring that changed my whole outlook (with a little help from hormone replacement). She said that any woman over fifty who has a body part that still looks good should be flaunting it every day. Her attitude made such an impression on me! She seemed so free and unencumbered, so alluring and sexy—what a dynamic presentation!

Around that time my husband and I were working with a female divorce mediator, which turned out to be fortuitous. Most of the meetings took place at my house, and she told me she was quite enamored of my decorating style. She decided to make it her mission to turn me into a professional interior decorator. With her relentless support and encouragement, I started my own business.

Slowly, I started to regain my bearings and equilibrium. As I began to work with clients and fulfill their expectations, I also began to realize my own goals. I had a renewed self-esteem and confidence, and soon a new hair color. Not long after, there was the occasional date. Within months, my business was flourishing and I was going out nearly every night.

To my surprise, I realized I was happier than I'd been in a long time. I had risen up like the phoenix, but little did I know I was about to be struck down again.

I had just turned sixty, even though I knew I didn't look it, when I wandered into a street fair in the upscale southern California neighborhood of Brentwood. As I strolled through the array of kiosks and booths a woman began frantically waving her arms in my direction.

"You! Come here!" she shouted.

Curious, I strolled toward her.

"Are you married?" she asked excitedly. I shook my head and she shoved a piece of paper under my nose. "I have got *so many* men," she cooed, "that would die to go out with you!" Now I realized she was running a booth for a dating service. "You're absolutely gorgeous! I'll have you married by the end of the year, I promise."

I was so pumped up by her pitch that I was already planning what designer would do my wedding gown.

"Let's get going," she squealed, pressing a pencil into

my hand. "Wait 'til you see how many wealthy bachelors I have for you!" I was mentally choosing my bridesmaids when she said, "By the way, how old are you?"

Batting my baby blues, I said, "Sixty."

The enthusiasm drained from her face, and she snatched the paper from my hand as if taking matches from a toddler.

"I can't help you," she said icily, taking back her pencil as well. "You're too old."

My self-esteem deflated like leaky balloon. Dazed, I wandered through the crowd with her words echoing in my head so loudly I was sure everyone else could hear them, too—"You're too old, you're too old, too old, old, old, old. . . ."

By the time I reached my car I was fighting back tears. I felt obsolete and invisible, as if I didn't deserve love or even happiness. Too old, old, old . . .

Then I got mad. Wait a minute, I thought, I haven't even peaked yet! And how many other women have been made to feel this way—even by members of their own sex? I knew then that I would make certain that this second part of my life would be just as fabulous—if not more so—as the first part.

This is no longer the world that Helen Gurley Brown described to us in her 1962 book, *Sex and the*

Single Girl. We believed the little mouseburger when she told us that being single was bliss. Perhaps so, but these days it's quite a bit more complicated and sometimes it's downright frightening. The world has changed and so has a woman's role in society. Women know a lot more now, but we need every iota of that knowledge to survive, and we need to share what we've learned.

If there's one thing I've learned, it's that once you're over the hill it's time to start picking up speed. You needn't give up everything that you once considered fun (including sex) just because you've hit another age marker. I realized that while life might not exactly begin at fifty, it most certainly doesn't come to a screeching halt—unless you let it. The sixty-year-old woman is still a viable force in today's world. She works, she dates, she is sexual, she is chic, and she is dynamic. It's not about being "beautiful" in the classic sense. Although it sounds like a cliché, it's about being beautiful inside. And *that's* all about being comfortable and confident in your own skin, being clear about who you are and what you want.

I made up my mind to share my wisdom and experience with other single women who have fallen victim to age discrimination in the most personal and devastating ways. I decided to write this book, and I knew the perfect collaborator. I first met Raechel Donahue in 1969. She was the embodiment of the woman of the times, a perfect combination of elegance and funk. Widowed in 1975, Raechel remained successfully single, gracefully breezing through romances and media careers. She was still a sexy dynamo in her fifties and I couldn't think of a better writing partner. We pooled our forty years of single life so that we could make yours more fun.

So kick off those practical shoes and get ready for what could easily become the *best* time of your life. You don't need a rocking chair. You just need to rock!

This book is to help you do just that. Older women need to know that they can still be glamorous, sensational, and sexy. They just need to know The Ropes.

How Old *Are* You Anyway?

Pros and cons of lying about your age

Age only matters if you're a cheese.

—HELEN HAYES

*L*ying about one's age is always a dilemma. Once you've done it, you're stuck with it, and more often than not it will come back to bite you in the most inappropriate place. Whenever possible, go with the truth.

I have a hideous compulsion to tell the truth about my age. Possibly because I think if age is going to be an issue, it should be on the table up front. That way there are no disappointments or surprises. Besides, if I lie about my age, I must also lie about what I've done in my life, and that would make me less of a person, if only to myself. Also, since I know I look younger than my age, I like invoking that look of shock, although I admit it's more fun to do it to women than to men.

The one time I tried to play it coy, the man fell for me hard. On our third or fourth date he started telling me how he had frozen some of his sperm and I was in deep soup when I realized he was planning for "our child." Oh, boy.

I was working on just exactly how I was going to break the news to him when he asked, "How old are you, anyway?"

First I made him guess. Bless his little tadpole heart, he guessed forty.

"Sixty," I said, batting my eyelashes.

He was just having a sip of champagne and, to his credit, he didn't do a spit take and no bubbles came out of his nose. But he was rendered speechless.

As for me, I spent the rest of the evening wallowing in the pleasure of looking forty.

It was our last date. I'll bet he asks that age question a lot earlier in the game from now on.

It's a big thrill when a man under guesses your age by twenty years, but when another woman does it, it's absolute bliss.

I was a guest at a cocktail party honoring one of my older daughter's friends, chatting with a group of people about the fact that we were all born during the war, when another woman joined the circle.

"I was born during World War II," she chimed in, shooting me a skeptical glance. "What war were *you* born in?"

"WWII, 1942," I chirped, meeting her gaze with my most ingenuous smile.

I can't really tell you her reply. It was muttered under her breath as she turned on her heel and walked away. Sometimes, as Dorothy Parker said, a girl's best friend is her mutter. In this case, the mutter was *my* new best friend.

I was waiting in an airport bar when a well-dressed woman remarked, apropos of almost nothing, that we appeared to be the same age. And we did, I agreed. In fact, I had noticed her when we were going through security and had thought the same thing myself.

"You haven't had anything done, have you," she said, as a statement rather than a question. I confessed to having a little Botox just recently. "How old *are* you anyway?" she then asked, not meaning it as an insult. It turned out that she was nearly ten years younger than I, which made me feel great and made her feel like heading for the nearest plastic surgeon.

I'm not interested in age. People who tell their age are silly. You're only as old as you feel.

— ELIZABETH ARDEN

While a man will fritter away his conversational time by bragging about how much money he makes, his golf score, or other more personal scores, a woman will cut directly to the chase. She doesn't need to tell anyone anything about herself; she just needs to know the other woman's age. Then she can compare herself and either get smug or take the whole day into the toilet.

What is it that makes some women come off as so much younger than others of the same age? To be sure, cosmetic surgery and taking care of yourself can help a great deal, but I have a friend who has had virtually every part of her body tucked, sucked, snipped, and sewn and she still looks every bit her real age! You know why? She doesn't do a lick of exercise and she has the posture of an old woman. Much of how you are perceived depends upon how you carry yourself. Remember, walk with your tail in the air!

On the other hand, I have friends who have done

nothing but soap and water for their fifty years on the planet and somehow still look ten years younger. I think a large part of how age looks on us is in the way we comfort ourselves. Once we stop having fun and start taking on those curmudgeonly attitudes, it's the beginning of the end of youth.

~~~~~~

We don't see things as they are; we see them as we are.

— ANAÏS NIN

Lying Up

If you approach your age with a sense of humor, even lying about it can be fun. While I don't advocate lying in any way, I know one funny woman who began what she calls "lying up" when she was in her late forties. "It was kind of like practicing for the next decade," she says. "I was forty-seven and I would tell people I was fifty, and they'd be amazed at how fabulous I looked!" It's amazing how the perception of age changes with just a few years—how could forty-seven be so different from fifty?

~~~~~~

The secret of staying young is to live honestly, eat slowly, and lie about your age.

— LUCILLE BALL

Of course, if you lie to make yourself older, you can easily and joyously go back to the truth. People may think you're weird, but their only question would be why someone would lie up. However, if you're saying you're younger than you are, you'd best take care to remember the fib and the accompanying birth years, graduation dates, and children's ages if you don't want to get caught.

Also, try to make the lie reasonable. It's no use pretending to be twenty-seven when you're really fifty-eight. Besides, who'd want to be that stupid again? See if you can figure out how old you are in the eyes of others. Don't ask your contemporaries because they can usually spot someone of their own generation a mile off. Try telling a young salesgirl at the cosmetic counter that you think that new lipstick shade is too young for you and then try to find out how old she thinks you are. Just know that even forty seems *really, really* old when you're in your twenties, so don't settle for a generalization; get the girl to commit to an actual number. If you get a guess that's ten years younger, then you're on the right track.

Sexy or Delusional?

Dressing like a teenager doesn't make you one, so don't do it. Perversely, if you dress like a granny, you'll definitely be perceived as one. And while there's certainly nothing wrong with having grandchildren, you don't have to advertise your age. If you're wearing a sweatshirt emblazoned with the slogan "Number One Grandma" you're pretty much advertising that you're out of the dating pool, lessening the odds that an attractive man will make a pass at you. I suppose you could try "This Granny Still Rocks!" but I'm not sure it'd make a big difference.

As shallow as it may sound, your clothes can make or break your image, at least in the eyes of others. How many tacky talk shows have you seen featuring a teenage girl desperately seeking a makeover for her superannuated Lolita mother? You know, the one who is wearing the see-through blouse that no one wants to see through? Tape one of those episodes and play it back every time you have an urge to dress like a dancer in an MTV video.

If you still have your micromini or (gasp!) hot pants, perhaps you could sell them on eBay as collectibles. Or donate those wild and crazy outfits to a thrift store and know that some young hottie will be channeling you as she wows the boys in a trendy nightclub while undulating to music that would give you a massive headache.

Use It or Lose It

You know you have to keep your body fit and supple as you get older, and you should give the same attention to your mind. Don't spend your evenings in front of the television. If you stay home, occupy your mind with something that makes you think—read a book, do a challenging crossword puzzle (the one in *TV Guide* doesn't count), or comb through the latest magazines for ideas on revamping your wardrobe or improving your life in general. Visit art galleries (especially the opening receptions when they serve wine and miniature quiches), go to a play, go to a rock concert, just go!

There's a difference between your chronological age and your *real* age. The way your body ages is directly related to the way you take care of yourself. No matter how good you look on the outside, you have to watch your cholesterol and blood pressure, as well as take care of your heart. Who cares how fabulous your face is if you drop dead at sixty? Take care of the whole package and you'll still be knockin' 'em dead at seventy-five.

In spite of the cost of living, it's still popular.

— KATHLEEN NORRIS

"How old *are* you anyway?" is the sort of back-handed compliment you must learn to relish as you hit the fifty and sixty signposts. For it most certainly is a compliment when someone recognizes that you have the verve and style of a much younger person and yet you emanate the power and wisdom that only comes (dammit!) with years of experience.

Suddenly Single

Adjusting to being alone

My husband said he needed more space.
So I locked him outside.

—ROSEANNE BARR

Whether it happens because of death or divorce, it's a shock to find yourself suddenly single after many years of marriage. The things that you took for granted—like him taking out the garbage—are suddenly gone, and you are responsible for twice as much of the minutiae of daily life. Unless you still have children at home, you realize you are now alone. And even with kids around, there are always those long nights.

I can only imagine the pain of being widowed, and my friends who have lost their husbands have spent years absolutely consumed by grief. I know my divorce devastated me, and my life was a mess for nearly five years. Perhaps that makes me sound pathetic, but adjusting to a single life and regaining my self-confidence was a tremendous struggle. As they say, you fall in love but you have to crawl out. My personal crawling episode lasted so long I was thinking of creating a line of designer kneepads.

Even if you're the one who initiated the divorce, it always comes as a shock to be single. And if you've been out of the loop for a decade or more, it can be tough to adjust to a new world of dating and solo survival. You need to get back in the game, so brush up on the ropes and suit up!

Start by taking a merciless inventory of your emotions. If you're beating yourself up, stop it, because nobody deserves self-inflicted injuries. You'll get enough bumps and bruises along the way without adding to the pain yourself. Go ahead and have a good cry to send off your past life and then start preparing to have the last laugh. As they say, living well is the best revenge, and it's up to you to make the life you want.

Have you seen Divorcée Barbie? She has a few wrinkles around the eyes, and she comes with all of Ken's stuff.

STEP ONE: FORGET HIM

It's important to make sure you're over your ex. No matter if the memories are good or bad, they're sure to sneak into your subconscious as if through a little trapdoor in your head. You have to replace them with something else and not necessarily a man. There are some surefire ways to accelerate the forgive-and-forget process, starting with the forgetting part. The forgiving often takes much longer. You know what they say: There are two sides to every divorce. Yours and the shithead's.

Wash Him Out of Your Hair . . . and Everything Else

First, get rid of anything that smells like him. Those pheromones are strong and they linger for a long time. It's true! Smell is perhaps the strongest and most persuasive of the senses, because it evokes memories even when you don't want to remember. Try not to see him for a few months unless you have to for some reason, such as shared child custody. It gets easier when you don't face him frequently, so obviously you should ditch the photos. You don't have to tear them up or burn holes in them where his lying, cheating head should be. You may not want to throw them away, so just put them in the basement until you're ready to be over him.

―――――――――――――――――――――――――――――――

For a single woman, preparing for company means wiping the lipstick off the milk carton.

— ELAYNE BOOSLER

Don't try to replace him right away. You've got plenty of time to be selective. Meanwhile, go and explore the outside world. Outside of your previous relationship, that is. Go out to lunch, visit a museum, go to a street fair, buy shoes (that always works and you know it). Oh, and redecorate your bedroom, with the emphasis on seduction, elegance, romance, and your own personal taste. At least you won't have your husband complaining that it's too feminine. If you don't have the budget to redecorate, try rearranging the furniture. It's sometimes enough to change the whole look of a room. Then perhaps add a different bedspread or a new lampshade. Little touches make the difference. Make that room (and the rest of your house) yours and you will be one step closer to a truly independent life.

STEP TWO: TAKE INVENTORY

Next, make a list of the good things that you already have (your health, your kids, your teeth, his car) and another list of possibilities for your new life (an eyelift, a yoga class, a younger boyfriend). Set your sights high for both lists, but especially for your future. It may sound trite, but the less negativity you project, the more receptive you'll be to positive happenings. There's little point in making a new life if it's going to be just like the old one except without a man or with a different one. This time around, make a vow to show off the nicest, smartest, prettiest version of yourself and before you know it, the role will fit you like a glove. To some degree, we are who we pretend to be. You don't have to put on airs or be phony, just shift your imagination into overtime and create a brand-new you. A really cool you.

We women are special creatures. While we may treasure moments of solitude, most of us fear loneliness, and we often associate that feeling with *being alone,* which is actually totally different. Just as you can be lonely in a crowd, you can also be completely alone without being lonely, and not just because you're schizophrenic and the voices in your head are keeping you company.

Women living alone represent more than half of one-person households.

In the years since my divorce, I have finally learned to enjoy my own company. In fact, it turns out that I'm one of my favorite people to hang out with. Think about it. Isn't it great to be with somebody who always wants to do exactly what *you* want to do? To go where *you* want to go? You are your own perfect companion, your own best friend, your buddy, and most trusted confidante. How lucky is that?

STEP THREE: PUT ON YOUR GAME FACE

This little trick of being alone with myself took me a few years to master. At first, I thought I would die from loneliness, especially during those times when my children were staying with their father. As I mention in the chapter called "Shall We Dance?" I sought out new ways to meet people. While that worked wonders for my social life, I did still feel lonely. It wasn't until I made myself realize that I was a strong, healthy woman with a great future ahead of me that I truly began to rebuild my life. I very much needed to celebrate all that I've learned and experienced in my long and full life. I'd had many happy years in my marriage, I was blessed with healthy children, I still had my sense of humor (although that took some doing), and I still looked pretty damned good, all things considered.

I went through my phone book and crossed out all the people who had dumped me after the divorce. Then I started to consider contacting some old friends who had not "chosen sides" but whom I had, thoughtlessly, ignored during my extended self-pity party. To my surprise, many of them were genuinely pleased to hear from me and some came right out and expressed delight that I had come out of my funk. I made time to go to lunch, to catch up, and to find out what was going on in the outside world that I'd been shutting out. Turns out it's a very interesting place that's absolutely rife with opportunity.

Is This Thing On?

I even decided to acquire some new skills. I'd been so busy being the perfect wife and hostess that I hadn't advanced into the world of technology. The only new electronic device I'd mastered was a toy of a more personal nature. So, I had my children teach me how to use the computer and learned the wonderful art of e-mail.

I'd always been sort of phobic about electronics, but then I realized that I could keep in touch with so many people and feel so much more creative than I would have if I'd just spent hours chatting on the phone.

───

I think, therefore I am single.

— LIZ WINSTON

And, of course, there was that brief episode of Internet dating, but we'll save that for the chapter called "The Dating Game."

Okay, so now you've got your game face on, it's time to get out on the field. You should think about whether you're looking to get married or just to start dating again (or possibly for the first time). Either way, there's lots of information in this book to help you out. But reading doesn't take the place of doing, my dears. As Auntie Mame declared, "Life is a banquet, and most poor suckers are starving to death!" It's time for you to start enjoying the repast and even to become a conspicuous consumer.

Tadpoling

The art of dating younger men

> *I'd rather be a babysitter than a nurse.*
> —IVANA TRUMP

*I*nstead of kissing a lot of frogs, mature women may prefer "tadpoles" (younger men). Don't call it cradle robbing—tadpoling is much cuter. Becky Fletcher of the *San Francisco Examiner* calls it "babysitting with perks." A group of spunky women in that forward-thinking city by the bay even declared National Tadpole Week, and they're lobbying to get this new definition of tadpole into the latest edition of Webster's dictionary. The verb "tadpole" would be the practice of women dating men who are ten or more years younger; the noun "tadpole" is that delightful creature, a man who is at least ten years his lover's junior.

So, are you tired of dating men your age who will

take you to a fabulous dinner but then nod off during the sex scene in the movies? There's no harm in having the best of both worlds. Get your expensive jewelry from the geezer and gorilla sex from the young stud muffin. Experience is highly overrated when it comes to lovemaking— enthusiasm and frequency make up for a lot!

When we are in our twenties and thirties, we design the man of our dreams and make a mental list of desirable attributes: We want him to be handsome, stylish, hard bodied, and successful. Our fantasy man must appreciate the finer things in life, like taking us to dinner and giving us jewelry. Oh, and he definitely has to be an imaginative, romantic lover.

But let's face facts. As the years go by, the list of requirements shrinks until we start thinking the best we can hope for in a man is that he's still breathing and doesn't miss the toilet when he pees. This, my darlings, might be the perfect time to consider the sport of tadpoling.

Here's to You, Ms. Robinson

Don't go thinking that this is a treat reserved for the rich, famous, or beautiful. There's a tadpole out there for every woman if only she would open her eyes and her mind. It's not that you should be trolling the nurseries or daycare facilities, but be receptive to the idea that you needn't limit your dating pool to the nearest rest home and that you very well could be considered attractive and sexy to a younger man. It's just possible that when that handsome young waiter (hoping to become an actor) complimented you on your legs he wasn't just angling for a bigger tip. He may have been trying to break the ice just as a man your own age would do.

Men have traditionally had to deal with the stigma of rejection, and it's no less a bummer to be shut down by someone older than by a twenty-something babe. Often the problem for the younger man is that he is unsure of how to approach an older woman. If he's tried it once or twice, he may have been shut down, particularly if he tried one of those lame pickup lines that we heard in our twenties. If he gets chucked under the chin or called "sonny" or some such motherly endearment, he's not going to pursue it further. More likely he'll be embarrassed and retreat to his den (depending upon his age, that might be his messy one-bedroom apartment).

A woman's always younger than a man at equal years.

— ELIZABETH BARRETT BROWNING

Back in the seventies, Burt Reynolds shocked the entertainment world when he appeared naked in *Cosmopolitan* magazine, his package discreetly tucked between his legs. Dinah Shore was pushing sixty when she took up with her thirty-something hunk and they flung themselves wholeheartedly into the scandalous love affair (oh, how easy it was to outrage people in those more innocent days). I was sitting near them at a dinner party after they first got together and I overheard her say to him, "Eat your vegetables, darling."

"I don't *want* to eat my vegetables," he replied petulantly.

Poor Dinah was on the cutting edge of the tadpole game and had apparently not yet learned to reign in her maternal instincts.

Older women are dignified. They seldom have a screaming match with you at the opera or in the middle of an expensive restaurant. Of course, if you deserve it, they won't hesitate to shoot you if they think they can get away with it.

— FRANK KAISER

What, you may be asking, is the value of having a relationship with a younger man rather than an older one? There's really not that much difference when you consider that men never really mature anyway. So the question should be instead, "What's the harm in it?"

To remodel an old joke:

A sixty-year-old woman tells her friend about the wild sex she's having with her thirty-year-old tadpole lover.

"My dear," asked her friend, "aren't you afraid that all that exertion might cause a heart attack?"

After a moment's consideration, the woman replies, "Well, if he dies, he dies!"

He who hesitates is a damn fool.

— MAE WEST

The mature woman may have trouble adjusting at first. After all, we are used to thinking the man should be at least a little older than the woman. That's old hat, darlings, and heaven knows we want the height of fashion in any hat, and the younger man is definitely in fashion. It's all over the gossip columns and magazine articles.

And there is certainly no lack of role models in the arena of dating younger men. Madonna pretty much invented the Boy Toy concept, but Cher carried on the tradition without ever settling down. And then there is Demi Moore and her twenty-something Ashton Kutcher. Rumor has it that he lied down about his age just to make the difference seem bigger! It's good to know that men are consistent when it comes to lying about the size of things.

Longtime May-December relationships abound in Hollywood, and who knows what lurks in the suburban bedrooms across the country. Susan Sarandon and Tim Robbins have weathered their twelve-year age difference; Mary Tyler Moore chose S. Robert Levine, eighteen years her junior after divorcing Grant Tinker; Raquel Welch gave it a try before dumping Richard Palmer (fifteen-year gap); and there were nineteen years separating Ralph Fiennes and Francesca Annis. Carol Burnett's husband Brian Miller was twenty-three years younger, but Joan Collins gets the Tadpoling Lifetime

Award for pushing the envelope with Percy Gibson with a whopping thirty-two-year discrepancy!

And that's just in America. Take a trip to Paris if you really want to see older women holding the reins. There, long-in-the-tooth lasses are prized for their glamour and their experience, in both life and the bedroom. They don't seem to be trying to hang on to their youth but rather to flaunt their maturity. Where else could an actress like Jean Moreau, with a face lined by years of living, prance around in a slip in her sixties and still be considered sexy? Heck, if she can do it, why can't we?

There's a Prince for You

It doesn't matter what you look like. Somewhere out there is a young man who finds you beautiful for all the right reasons. There's no need for you to dress provocatively or behave like a siren. A good tadpole appreciates the older woman's wisdom, confidence, and mature view of life. He knows she understands that life doesn't have to be taken seriously all of the time and that a good laugh is preferable to high drama. (Oh, and a sense of humor doesn't mean you tell him jokes. It means you laugh at his.)

With any luck you'll be at your most financially stable, have the most free time to spend making yourself look and feel fabulous, and have the confidence and flair that many younger (and older) men find compelling. It's up to you to use those assets to your best advantage.

If you're a widow who's collected on a large life insurance policy or a divorcée with a hefty settlement, your first instinct might be that he's after your money. If you are fortunate to be very, very wealthy, this might be a genuine issue, but generally it's only a small fraction of the attraction. While the younger man might appreciate a woman who can pull her own weight, that doesn't mean he's out to drain your bank account and turn your relationship into something that ends up on *Unsolved Mysteries*. Not that you should make him privy to your finances—quite the opposite—but you needn't let suspicion rule your sex life. After all, you're probably not looking to marry the guy, nor he you, so why not have a little fun even if you do pick up your share of the tab? There's no harm in going Dutch, but let's remember that the situation changes if you start paying for everything.

The main result of feminism has been the Dutch treat.

— NORA EPHRON

One younger man I've dated (he's twenty years my junior) said that he likes going out with me because I'm smarter than women his age. He's a well-educated historian and let's face it, I've lived more history than most of the women he dates have even read about. He finds it intriguing that I can talk about World War II and that I can quote Dorothy Parker. He's also an old-movie buff, and once we start talking about black-and-white films, the years between us fade away.

He says that he finds I am less demanding about where we go and what we do. At first I took this to mean that he thought I was a pushover. Then I realized that when I was younger I *was* more demanding, especially about less important things like which movie or restaurant we chose. Oddly, it would seem I was less demanding in crucial areas, such as character and substance in the men I dated. It was more important that he brought flowers than that he have a brain or a conscience.

Don't get me wrong, but that brain thing can be totally overrated. Ignorance really can be bliss at times. While you may not like 'em big and stupid, it can be a lot less taxing to sleep with a dumb guy than to try to have a real relationship with a smart guy who has a lot of baggage. And speaking of baggage, younger men tend to have less of it, especially the ones who are looking to date an older woman. Of course, there will be those with ex-wives and alimony payments, but often they are those terminal bachelors who haven't been able to settle down just yet. As long as you're not committed to making him commit, everything should go fine.

Older people exude bundles of sexuality. Older men and women tend not to run around like cats and dogs in heat.

— JACQUELINE BISSET

You need to watch out for your own luggage as well. Baggage is something we all carry, but there is no reason to share it with the man you're romancing, no matter his age. He doesn't want to hear about who else you've slept with, and he most certainly doesn't want to hear about how tough your life has been. Before he unzips his pants, you'd better zip your lip.

Lest it all sound too rosy, let's discuss just what younger men *don't* like about older women. Surprisingly, it doesn't have anything to do with what we look like. Generally, we look a whole heck of a lot better than the men our age and often just as good as men ten or even fifteen years younger. And if we work at it, we can look at least as good as any woman ten years our junior.

What men abhor can be summed up in one word: *bitterness*. Bitterness is not at all attractive. Some women are resentful about the way they were treated in the past, about not having a husband or about real or imagined slights in their careers or social lives. Sometimes it's that they never had the chance for a really steamy affair. So, now's the perfect opportunity. And as the saying goes, when opportunity knocks, answer the door naked.

And the trouble is, if you don't risk anything, you risk even more.

— ERICA JONG

It's most important to remember that you are, as it was said in that wonderful movie *Calendar Girls,* in the full flower of your womanhood. I say get busy getting pollinated before you go to seed!

How young should your tadpole be? The seven-year rule is a pretty good yardstick: Pick a man who is half your age plus seven. That means when you're sixty you can feel comfortable going out (or just sleeping with) a thirty-seven-year-old man. And if someone even younger approaches you, don't be afraid to bend the rule. I'm big on rule bending, but the one rule that never goes out the window is this: I never date any man whose mother is younger than I am.

It's important to tread carefully on that fine line that separates the joyous tadpoler from the predatory old bag looking to hang on to her youth. Avoid that trap by remembering that you're not necessarily looking to fall in love, just a roll in the hay. If it becomes something more, then you have cause to celebrate.

Do Tadpoles Have Legs?

Actually, research shows that tadpoling is not always just about the sex. There's a level of fun attached in spirited conversations, and younger people tend to be more passionate about their opinions. The tadpole will complain less about being "dragged" to the theater to see, say, *Urinetown,* and will most certainly be more willing to go for new experiences. What are the odds you'll get that older fuddy-duddy dentist boyfriend to try indoor rock climbing with you? Or doing anything after 10:00 P.M.?

~~~~~~

Plenty of guys are good at sex, but conversation, now there's an art.

— LINDA BARNES

Lest you think this is all just a flash in the pants, there is evidence that tadpole relationships actually tend to have legs, most lasting around ten years, and the average age difference is about thirteen years. According to Becky Fletcher, who is too young for tadpoling but nevertheless wrote an article about it, there's little fear that your young stud will dump you for some pretty young thing. Nope, turns out it's the older woman who usually breaks it off. Probably because he's gotten too old for her.

U.S. women outnumber men in every age group over thirty.

And maybe, just maybe, tadpoling can be good for your health and well-being—and not just because you'll be getting more exercise. Statistics show that there are more than three times the number of single women over sixty than bachelors in the same age group. The younger pool of single men is much larger, nearly the same as the older women group. And since men tend to die younger than women, it might just mean that if the relationship has longevity, you and your significant tadpole will die at the same time. Preferably in the sack.

It's Not Over 'Til the Fit Lady Swings

Exercise can change your life

> *The best exercise is sex. Unfortunately, you have to be in good shape to do it really well.*
>
> —LOIS CHARLES

The dead giveaway for the older babe is the butt. If your ass melts into your thighs, creating one indistinguishable flat slab, you've got Old Lady Caboose. The best way to get a good-looking ass is to get off yours!

There are a couple of other places where the aging gods strike particularly cruel blows. How did that little blob of fat between the arm and chest get there? You know, the one that makes sleeves a requisite? Learn to work your pectoral and chest muscles, and not only can you tighten up that pesky bit of flab, but it'll keep your boobs from sagging to your waist. And although it's literally all behind you, you may be aware of a couple of unattractive bulges surrounding the back strap of your bra. Throw a little extra work into your back and you can lose the extra flesh while improving your posture, which will keep you from that unpopular hunchback look.

People have remarked to me on numerous occasions that I am a strong woman. I guess they meant my character, but I never really got the feeling of what it means to be strong until I started weight training at fifty-seven. Talk about a late bloomer. Sadly, I didn't get serious about my body until I was in my fifties. This is not to say that I didn't work out: I dutifully followed workout trends like a well-toned sheep. I was pummeled and pampered at the elite ladies retreat, The Sanctuary, where the theme of the exercise class seemed to be "tense your buttocks, ladies." I bent with Bikram yoga, burned with Jane Fonda's Workout, and I was doing Pilates in the seventies, when it was still an arcane discipline practiced only by celebrity devotees behind closed doors. I did the twenty-minute Nautilus routine, and paid through the nose for private sessions with a Hollywood exercise guru who turned out to be less interested in the development of my muscles than the development of his script.

Now I've finally come to understand what my body needs, how it works, and how best to keep it tuned like a fine instrument. I've discovered that even if you're willing to work for it, you must make the commitment to be consistent and practice perfect form. If you've stayed in shape, it's time to accelerate your workout a bit. If your womanly curves have turned into waving flags, you can still get it all back. It just takes discipline, and the all-important weight-bearing exercise. At first I thought I was going to collapse before I could finish even ten repetitions, but after a few weeks I developed the concentration and stamina, followed by a noticeable increase in actual strength.

Three hours of moderate exercise per week reduces blood estrogens and the risk for breast cancer in postmenopausal women.

When you're in control of weight sufficiently heavy to require digging into the core of all your muscles simultaneously, that is a true feeling of strength. It's like the mother that lifts a 2,000-pound automobile off her child—you don't know you have the strength until it's called for. In my case, I was lifting a one-ton weight from my spirit.

To my amazement, when I started to apply that

same feeling of strength to mental exercises (like raising teenagers by myself), I realized that the connection between a strong mind and strong body is seamless. And you have to exercise them both to keep them supple, strong, and, of course, sexy.

Work Out Baby, Work Out

Some women like to hike up hills and mountains for exercise. The only thing I like to hike up is my skirt. For exercise, I prefer the air-conditioned comfort of a gym.

Joining a gym (or anything else, for that matter) is a problem for some women. Many don't like the social aspect of the whole thing, the need to wash your hair and put on mascara both before and after your workout, not to mention the color-coordinated workout clothing. All that stuff takes up valuable time, energy, and cash. Others just shudder at the idea of getting sweaty while perched on turquoise vinyl—it's a bit too much like having sex in a fifties diner.

I maintain that the best place for a workout is a serious gym, like the worldwide Gold's Gym chain, where weight lifters gather to compare pecs. The testosterone in the air is bound to give your spirits a lift, and it's a wonderful opportunity to appreciate man at his most beautiful and self-absorbed. The display of male pulchritude can make the workout a lot more pleasant. There's certainly no harm in looking. Just don't expect them to be looking at you. Many of them are too muscle-bound to even turn their heads, and they're probably more interested in admiring themselves in the mirror.

Sixty percent of Americans do not exercise at all.

But the gym really is the easiest way to get in shape, especially if you use a trainer, at least in the beginning. Most gyms have trainers available, and for as little as twenty bucks a session, it's worth it to learn how to do your exercises properly. It's kind of like psychiatry: It works better if you pay for it. It's easy to blow off a schedule you've set for yourself, but you'll think twice about canceling with your trainer. To begin with, it's always that same day of the workout that you don't want to do it, so you'd have to pay anyway. Worse, if you make it for the next session, the trainer will heap scorn upon you. And probably double your weights. Guilt, shame, and money are great motivators, at least in the realm of physical fitness.

For some women, the term *personal trainer* has a whole different meaning, with heavy emphasis on the "personal" aspect.

I have a friend who had a hot-and-heavy fling with her hunky trainer, and when they broke up she ended up having to go to a completely different gym miles from her home to avoid running into him every single day. That, my dears, is certainly not worth it.

If you're already in pretty good shape but feel you should kick it up a notch, try doing it literally with a kickboxing class. You don't actually have to kick another person, but you can most certainly relieve some aggression and frustration by knocking the stuffing out of a heavy bag. It's a complete body workout and when you're done you'll be as sweaty and depleted as if you've had marathon sex. Many gyms offer a combination of kickboxing and self-defense that will increase your confidence and get you in such shape that even your wimpiest date will never worry about having sand kicked in his face, at least while you're by his side.

If working out in a coed situation makes you uncomfortable, try a women's gym. There's a certain freedom that comes when you're sweating with the girls. Plus, since you don't have to worry about how you look in your workout clothes, you can wear a bodysuit so that you can really see the effects of your exercises. Of course, you can see all your flaws as well, but that can serve as an incentive to work harder to correct them.

The Hard Body Starts at Home

So you're not a gym-rat type, and your idea of exercise is thumbing through the tabloids in the supermarket line. Yeah, well, how many star fitness articles have you breezed through that stress the importance of weight-bearing exercise to prevent osteoporosis? It's a constant femme feature on talk shows, even though usually demonstrated by an impossibly fit yoga/Pilates instructor to the stars. You read about celebrities who work out for two hours a day, and you wonder just exactly where you could find two hours to do anything private, much less something as painful as exercise. Remember, creating a hard body is part of the movie star job description, something that they often shell out hundreds of thousands of dollars to create. But the box-office babe's six-pack abs are going to be scaled up for display on a fifty-foot movie screen, whereas you only have to look fit in a mirror that reflects your actual size. On that level, fitness is all about perspective.

Once you accept that you're not going to have Demi

Moore's body unless you have a whole lot of free time and the incentive of millions of dollars to create it, then the task is much easier. All that you need to do is to make the strongest, tightest, most beautiful body that you can, within the constraints of your time and monetary budgets. You may not get paid millions of dollars, but the paycheck will come in the form of self-esteem and compliments from people who care about you. Plus, you won't have to put up with the pesky paparazzi.

The best thing about working out at home is that you don't have to spend a dime on workout getups. In fact, exercising naked is a great motivator. A surefire method for staying in shape is housework, particularly if you do it in the buff. While loading the dishwasher may not actually do much to build muscles, there's nothing quite like leaning over to clean the bathroom sink and getting a good look at your naked body to give you a bit of inspiration. If every stroke of the broom sets the flab on your upper arms waving, you'll get the message as if delivered by the semaphore flags your triceps so tragically resemble. When you bend over to bag up the trash do you see your stomach or your feet? If you can't see your feet, maybe you ought to get on them and try walking to the grocery store instead of driving.

The basic idea is to try to use every muscle every

day. Start by carefully stretching your back and neck. Do it slowly, like your lover should, reaching out and making yourself as tall as you can.

Who knew that someone would actually have to say, "Don't forget to breathe!"? As it turns out, breathing is key in proper exercise. Try this for starters: Breathe in through your nose (this fills your diaphragm) until you can't take in any more air. Lift your shoulders up to your ears and then pull them back as far as you can, as if you could make them touch. Blow the air out your mouth, emptying your lungs, and drop your shoulders and arms straight down—that is your perfect posture and the core of your balance. Generally speaking, you should breathe out at the beginning of the exercise movement and in again as you return to your starting point.

If you are totally new to the workout world, you might investigate learning the breathing techniques by taking one of those introductory yoga classes you will find offered by community centers or the YWCA. It's not like you have to go there every day, but it's good to get some ideas before you begin your homegrown workout program.

Yoga, by the way, is easy to do at home while you're waiting for your hair to dry or to find out who's sleeping with whom on your favorite soap. Also, positions like "Downward Dog" are very sexy homework.

Walk the Walk

My absolute favorite exercise is walking. Not only can it be done almost anywhere, it's much easier on the knees. Also, studies show that older people who are consistent walkers have more alert brains and are less prone to dementia. That alone is enough to keep me in step.

I had a girlfriend with whom I used to walk my neighborhood. We were the self-appointed "Beauty Patrol," tracking new additions, gardening ideas, paint jobs, and eyesores. Once bitten by a loose dog, she carried a golf club with her at all times to ward off aggressive canines.

After a while we started walking up the biggest hill backward. It gave us a new view, and what a great burn for the glutes and thighs!

One final benefit of our daily strolls came when I saw a woman with a massage table coming out of an enormous and lovely home. I got her card as she was getting into her car and she turned out to be the best masseuse I'd ever had. I used her for years, and it was all because of those daily walks.

Walking in groups is great fun, especially in groups of women. Talking as you walk helps you breathe properly and keep a comfortable pace. There are bunches of women around the country who have discovered a novel way to make their walks entertaining. They walk the malls in groups! Not only are they safely indoors, sheltered from sun or storm, but they get to window-shop while they walk. Now, *that's* a productive workout.

Smart Women Love Dumbbells

Just like at the gym, your home workout should include the all-important weight-bearing exercise. This will not only tone your body, but can keep you from looking like the witch in *Snow White* by preventing osteoporosis. And it's easy to get started at home. Smart women can make use of dumbbells, and not just the ones you meet at Starbucks.

Start with a pair of five-pounders, which you can get at a discount drugstore chain rather than some expensive sporting-goods store. You can buy heavier ones when you feel you've outgrown the baby weights. Do slow bicep curls in front of the mirror, and then straighten your arms and try to touch the backs of your hands to each other behind your back for a good triceps workout. Do as many as you can, then rest a minute or two and do another set. Then try to touch your toes with the weights. When you get down there, swing your weights in small circles, stretching out your neck and shoulders, ten circles clockwise, ten counterclockwise. Touch the ends of the weights together and slowly come up from the floor, drawing your hands up the front of your body as if pulling a zipper up a very tight (and somewhat risqué) gown, one you can imagine yourself wearing once you're in perfect shape. Repeat the whole routine two more times. Then strap on some ankle weights and do two dozen reverse leg lifts on each side, then repeat, just to make sure you have your ass covered, as it were.

Even these tame and easy home exercises can make all the difference, but it's vital that you do them religiously. You really need to get at least thirty minutes of exercise every day, even if you don't do it all at once. Ten minutes in the morning before you start your day, ten minutes at lunchtime, and ten minutes at the end of the day, and you won't even notice it cutting into your time. However, you'll notice it cutting back your appetite and perking up your derriere.

There are other vital muscles that needs exercising,

and they're right between your legs. The vaginal and pelvic muscles need to be in shape to prevent you from peeing your pants every time you cough or sneeze. Isolate the vaginal muscle you want by trying to stop mid-stream when you're on the toilet. If you can manage that, then you know what muscle to exercise. Then exercise that muscle by squeezing and releasing. Do it for five minutes a couple of times a day. This exercise is called the Kegel, named after Dr. Arnold Kegel, who invented it for women who were candidates for difficult childbirth. You can do it any time and anywhere since no one can see the action you're creating. Then all you have to do is anticipate any motion that might cause you to spring a leak. Hold the squeeze until after you sneeze! Or cough, or jump, or lift something heavy. Keep it up and you'll not just be saving yourself the humiliation of wearing Depends, but your lover will discover that you have a whole new way to hold on.

Whether it's yoga, spinning, Jazzercise, running—whatever—find a reason to use your body in order to keep it fluid. We seasoned chickies have lived long enough to realize that the "use it or lose it" theory is valid. And you have more to lose than just your body; your self-respect is tied to your self-image. As the saying goes, you're only as pretty as you feel. And you'll feel a whole lot prettier if you're in good shape.

And remember, after you've built this gorgeous new body for yourself, no matter how good you look, there are still two things it is never wise to do while naked: fry bacon and use power tools.

Romance in the Dark

Tips and tricks for the boudoir

After we made love, he'd take a piece of chalk and outline my body.

—JOAN RIVERS

Hey, we may be getting closer to sixty but we're not six feet under. Perhaps not all of us are willing to bare our bodies on the beach, but as long as we keep our trysts indoors, we can pretty much control how good we look. Besides, it's the stuff that happens when his eyes are closed that really counts— and that sort of thing can be enhanced only by our level of experience.

First there is the lighting issue. Candles, we all know about candles. Scented ones, even better. This doesn't mean you can't have soft light from a lamp, but do remember that backlight is much more favorable, even if only from the television. Your lovely silhouette can be etched in his mind, and without the wrinkles, too.

Ninety-six percent of candles are bought by women.

Oh, and speaking of wrinkles (and let's not do so too often), it just so happens that one of the most flattering positions for the older woman is flat on her back. Now, tell me *that's* not a happy coincidence! One note of caution: Even though the supine position makes for a smooth face, you may find your breasts in your armpits.

Grooming Is the Better Part of Valor

A woman who knows The Ropes realizes that flawless grooming is essential to a romantic and exciting tryst. The legs must always be smooth, the pubes neatly trimmed or bleached or dyed or whatever looks the best. Look at it this way: If it's all turned white already, it'll be much easier to dye! Probably best to leave the hot pink to the younger, pierced set, though.

It goes without saying (or it should) that your hair should be clean and coiffed, your nails neat and clean, and every inch of your body moisturized. And that means all the time, not just on date night. For starters, you never really know when a chance meeting with someone you've been flirting with will turn out to be something more. You don't want to have to excuse yourself because your legs are so prickly you could win a wrestling match with a porcupine. Remember when your mom used to remind you to wear clean underwear in case you got into an accident? Well, wear sexy underwear and keep the body pristine in case you're rescued from that accident by a handsome attorney with a home nearby where you can rest until you've collected yourself (and your settlement, for it surely wasn't *your* fault).

Underwear doesn't really begin to describe the range of possibilities for sexy, intimate garments. You don't have to have a Victoria's Secret body to wear glamorous lingerie, and even if you could get that thin, you'd probably look like a bag of elbows. Besides, most of us spent our youth trying to find panties that *wouldn't* ride up the crack, and now butt floss is all the rage. The only thong you need is the pearl version, which you won't find in a department store. Go for a high-end lingerie shop for this beauty: a bit of flat, stretchy lace supporting a single or double strand of sturdy faux pearls running from stem to stern. Not only does the very look of it drive men to distraction but it has the added advantage of clitoral stimulation. One woman said she brought it on a second-honeymoon cruise and, after trying it on, she told her husband he might as well turn in, as she didn't need him anymore.

Brevity is the soul of lingerie.

— DOROTHY PARKER

Believe it or don't, not all men are turned on by exotic lingerie. It even scares some of them. The pearl thong is bordering on kinky, to be sure, but not if properly presented. We are at an age where we can pull off a floor-length satin nightgown with a lace top. Sheer elegance, waiting for what's beneath to be revealed. You may have to lay out a hundred bucks at a proper lingerie store to get something that supports your breasts, flatters your behind, and moves like the summer wind, but it will last for a decade if you take care of it. And it will, in turn, take care of you.

Simply put, it's time to let go of the bustier and tap pants and go for long, flowing, and classically sexy. You don't need a lot of money to make this happen. Try an "experienced clothing" store, a place where the wealthy turn in their (often never worn) discards. Try a Goodwill store in a well-to-do neighborhood for amazingly great bargains for a woman who knows quality when she sees it. Look at the labels for the designer and the fabric content and you may find yourself with an expensive peignoir for a pittance.

Don't forget the feet! The shoes we choose—especially the truly sexy ones—all too often punish our feet. Also remember that there are nerve endings in your feet, so massaging them gives the rest of your body some benefit as well. Every time you get out of the shower or bath you should pumice your feet, paying special attention to calluses and corns, and then slather those hardworking puppies with a heavy lotion or thick cream. That's the time to don those thick, ugly gym socks we don't want to be seen in outside of, well, the gym. The socks will keep you from sliming your satin sheets and won't really soak up too much of the emollient. Your tootsies will be soft as silk and once you put a coat of polish on your toes, you're good to go, girl. Do this faithfully and you can save enough pedicure cash to buy a nice bottle of champagne.

Setting the Stage

Now that you've attended to your appropriate body parts, it's time to look at the playing field—your bedroom. It should be a luxurious, inviting cocoon, not a repository for dirty clothes or a hiding place for all the junk you can't bear to throw away but have no room to store. And while you may like to work in bed, stash that pile of papers in the nightstand. Oh, yes, your children and/or grandchildren are adorable, but find another place to hang their photographs. Ditto for pictures of you cavorting in some resort with your ex- or late husband(s). If a fling turns into something permanent, there will be plenty of time to share your memories. Meanwhile, let this be a room for present romance, not a shrine to your past.

Men prefer white bedrooms; women like blue ones.

This is your *boudoir,* and it should be a delight to the senses. Ditch the collection of stuffed animals and the two dozen cutesy ruffled throw pillows. I always like velvet drapes in my bedroom so I can create darkness on demand. Not only is this handy for an afternoon tryst, but vital on those rare mornings I get the chance to sleep late. A variety of colors are available everywhere from Pottery Barn to Target as well as any number of catalogues. Pick something that adds a little drama to the room and don't forget to measure from the pole to the floor. You don't have to make it look like

Mata Hari's mantrap, but it should convey your sensuality while still feeling comfortable for a man. You may fit perfectly in that four-poster canopy bed with the high headboard and footboard, but if you like a tall partner, you might consider swapping out for a king-sized venue.

You've probably heard about feng shui, the practice of rearranging your decor to create positive energy. You may think it's a lot of hooey, but when it comes to the bedroom, it seems more logical. Mirrors, sensual sounds, candles, and fresh flowers figure into the positive feng shui of the boudoir. Negatives include junk, games, dirt, storage, and dead plants (dead anything, actually, but we hope that won't be an issue for you). Make a point of keeping those things out of your bedroom, unless, of course, you want to have a dead-end relationship with a game-playing loser who has a load of past issues. Experts in the field say that if you put something red on or under your bed your sex life will heat up. Imagine how much it would heat up if the red thing is something silky that you're wearing.

Okay, so you're thinking, what's the point? Your bedroom has been an action-free zone for quite some time. Maybe you're just not making it possible. Let's face it, if you know your bedroom is littered with candy wrappers and three days' worth of clothes you've dropped on the floor, you're not exactly in the mood to bring someone there for a night of wild abandon. Even if the opportunity presents itself, you'll turn it down, giving yourself and your suitor a series of stupid excuses. You have nobody to blame but yourself if you want love but don't create a pleasant place in which to invite it. If your love nest is more like a rat's nest, you'll get the corresponding results.

I am a marvelous housekeeper. Every time I leave a man, I keep his house.

— ZSA ZSA GABOR

Now, this may sound weird, but make sure your closet is orderly. Let's say he (yikes!) actually decides to spend the night and wants to hang up his clothes. Even if he's the kind of guy who usually uses his Exercycle as a coatrack, he'll make some assumptions about you if your closet looks like a pack-rat's nest. Make sure there's a handy little clear space on one end of the closet pole and line your sexiest shoes up on the shelf above, where they'll be sure to meet his eye. Then hang a slinky nightgown on the wall hook right next to where he'll be stashing his duds. It'll work wonders for his imagination.

Your imagination is important here, too. Not only is it okay to fantasize about having sex with Tom Cruise or the entire NFL (teams of your choice), it can rev up your sex drive. Scoff if you must about romance novels, but it's a fact that reading a bodice ripper can have a positive effect on a woman. A couple of paperbacks with Fabio on the cover and your pheromone output just might go into overdrive.

Women who read romance novels have 74 percent more sex.

On to the bathroom! While this smaller room might not immediately conjure up romance, consider that if you don't want yours to go in the toilet, you'd better make sure it's an attractive place to perform the necessary cleanup activities as well as routine bodily functions. Of course, everything must be squeaky clean, there must be a full roll of toilet paper, and plenty of small and large towels. But you also must stash most of your personal grooming items: no visible razors, tooth-whitening strips, douche bags, hormone pills, or cosmetics. And don't think that women are the only ones who snoop in medicine cabinets. Keep the cold-sore medicines, yeast infection creams, and prescription drugs in an attractive Oriental box or under the sink. Any man who looks under your sink had better be a plumber.

You Are a Goddess

In the end, your sexuality is all up to you, as is your sex life. Women are the eternal element of creation, and not just because our bodies can bear children. In all of recorded time, we have been artists' models and their muses, the ideal of beauty. There's nothing to be gained by sitting on the couch and munching cookies while wishing you were the heroine in a romance novel. You are the heroine, and the romance is there for the taking. After all, as Aristotle Onassis said, "If women didn't exist, all the money in the world would have no meaning."

Although there are many things we can't control in our lives, we do have options every day. A bad-hair day can be fixed with a fabulous hat, a pimple can be transformed into a temporary beauty mark. Whether you want a fabulous single sex life or a long-term romance, you must create a complete environment, a display in which it can flourish. And since you are the centerpiece of the display, you must give yourself the care and nourishment that a flower in full bloom needs and deserves.

Age is not an issue, darlings. We are women, and whether we realize it or not, we run the world. Orson Welles said that man created civilization in order to impress his girlfriend. Now, that's some kind of power.

It's all up to you: Feeling sexy will undoubtedly translate into looking sexy. If you believe you're unattractive, how can anyone see that you are beautiful? That's not just about your superficial appearance, either. It's the way you *look*. As in *at* someone. If you've forgotten how to throw a smoldering glance, read the chapter called "The Dating Game."

The Skinny on Skin

Pointers for maintaining your skin

> *I'm tired of all this nonsense about beauty being only skin-deep. That's deep enough. What do you want, an adorable pancreas?*
>
> —JEAN KERR

I have always received a lot of compliments on my skin, and even after passing my sixtieth birthday I still get rave reviews. While I've always believed that much of it is due to the fact that I was blessed with good skin genes, at my age that is no longer something I can rely on, and neither should you. From now on, it's all about how I take care of my skin.

If you haven't taken good care of your skin up to now, it's really not too late to start. You don't have to spend a lot of money or even a lot of time but you do have to be consistent. I have only three basic skin-care rules: exfoliate, moisturize, and protect. Skin technology is quite advanced these days, and there are plenty of products to choose from regardless of your budget.

Women spend an average of fifty-five minutes grooming each day.

The quickest path to good skin is the one that takes you out of the sun. Put on sunscreen anytime you even think about going outside. Of course, we all know how good we look with a tan, but the payback, as you've probably already discovered, is a bitch: wrinkles, spots, and skin cancer. Tanning creams and lotions are the only safe way to go these days. I like the Clarins gel myself because it goes on smoothly and doesn't get blotchy. By the way, don't fool yourself into thinking a tanning bed will save you from looking like an apple doll, because it won't. Your skin will still get damaged.

Except for special occasions when I want to look as if I've just returned from a week in the Bahamas, I don't care for the spray-on tan, but I have a friend who swears by it. She was a sun worshipper for years and has some of those nasty spots on her arms and legs, but she's developed a pretty neat trick. She puts concealer on the spots before going for her spray session and everything evens out. However, even though the spray method doesn't require much effort, you have to stay out of the swimming pool, or the tan will bleach off in a most unattractive pattern. And it also dries the skin terribly, so keep slathering on the moisturizer.

Forty-one percent of all women use body and hand moisturizers three times a day.

Whatever method you choose, just don't take it so far that you look like George Hamilton. If you can't tell when you're too tan, then you're in danger of succumbing to tanorexia.

Take It Off; Take It All Off!

Exfoliation is crucial, both for the face and the body. You can use a simple oatmeal scrub if you're concerned about cost, and you can even make your own. Or, you can get a slightly more radical effect by using a moisturizer with alpha hydroxy acid or a cream with a retinol base. Retinol is a nighttime thing, however, so don't wear it out in daylight. Also be aware that alpha hydroxy acids, depending upon the concentration, can irritate the skin, so be sure to test any product on a small area before using it all over your face. Generally, even if you don't get a major irritation, AHA can make your skin a bit red when you first use it, but after a time you'll get a nice glow. The point is to get those dead skin cells off your face. If you have the money, go to your dermatologist for a monthly beta lift. It resurfaces the skin and removes fine lines with no downtime whatsoever.

Legend has it that Doris Day used to coat her body in Vaseline before bed.

Exfoliating the entire body is very simple. Use a firm (not hard), natural bristle brush to go over your entire body *before* you get into the shower or bath. A favorite of some opera singers treated by a masseuse friend of mine is a bath made with a cup of nonfat dried milk (lactic acid), crushed rose petals, and a few drops of eucalyptus oil. You'll step out of the tub with a renewed glow and baby-soft skin. This gives you a reason to save rose petals and your skin at the same time. Coincidentally, this inexpensive, easily accessible combination is very similar in composition to a very pricey assortment of products available only through dermatologists, and can render similar results.

If you're serious about repairing and/or maintaining your skin, find a really good dermatologist. The advances made in skin technology are awesome, but most of them are only available through a medical doctor. I personally prefer a very high-tech routine for my skin care. My dermie makes it his business to stay informed about the latest, cutting-edge products on the market for skin care. There are two items in particular that I think render dramatic results: moist pads and serum. There are two compounds, one used in the morning, one in the evening. The morning version, Multi HA MAX pads, has 10 percent glycolic acid, 10 percent lactic acid, and 5 percent salicylic acid. The pads are used to give the skin a good sloughing, taking off the fine lines and generally refreshing the surface of the face. I follow that with Prevage, the most powerful antioxidant available. At night, I use the other pad, KojiLac-CHQ (4 percent hydroquinone), which is used as a skin lightener, very helpful with those dreadful brown spots and the uneven color of the skin, followed by retinol serum, which is retin A taken to the extreme. These products can be obtained only from your dermatologist or your cosmetic surgeon and Prevage does not require a prescription. It can be used alone as a high-tech moisturizer, but can give a more effective result when used in conjunction with the pads. In general, this program gives me a smooth, soft, even texture, and color that belies my chronological age.

The average woman has seventeen square feet of skin, and all of it needs special care.

Those with oily skin may have spent their younger years cursing blackheads and blemishes, but they'll thank their lucky stars as they get older. Their dry-skinned sisters may be plagued with fine wrinkles while they themselves retain a plumper, more moist skin well into their fifties. If you do still have blackheads, it's a good idea to have them extracted by getting a professional cleansing facial. Whatever you do, don't squeeze those pesky things yourself. Leave it to the pros.

Go ahead and spend the fifty bucks that you would have spent on a pair of trendy running shoes. Get it done one time and then maintain it yourself by steaming your face with a warm washcloth, thoroughly cleansing and finishing up with a good mask at least once a week. Once the blackheads are removed, the pores have a chance to close up and your skin will be smoother.

Hair Today, Gone Tomorrow

The older a woman gets, the more it seems that her eyebrows attempt to relocate to her chin. No matter how well you care for your skin it's all for naught if it's covered with hair. It's a good bet that the last thing a man wants to feel as he leans in for that romantic kiss is the stubble on your chin.

For those with dark facial hair, the best way to go is permanent laser removal. It's not that expensive, and I think it's worth almost any amount of money just to avoid the paranoia that your chin could suddenly sprout a cluster of coarse black hairs when you don't have an opportunity to remove them.

There are other, less expensive, temporary remedies. Depilatories and waxing are effective, but there's always that dreadful transitional period when the hair can be seen just before it breaks through the skin. It's not long enough to remove, but it looks like a blackhead about to erupt. Ick. I say get out your credit card and run to the nearest laser.

Although you would think that blondes would have it easier, light hair presents a different problem. Blonde or white hair does not attract the light of a laser beam and therefore renders the process useless.

What to do? I suggest a very bright halogen desk lamp, a 7X magnifying mirror, and very good tweezers. I consider my twenty-five-dollar Tweezerman among my most prized possessions and my best defense against an approaching goatee. Whatever you do, don't even *think* about shaving your face. Ever. It could easily become one of the biggest mistakes of your grooming career.

The Eyes Have It

While my Italian heritage gave me a terrific head of hair (and quite a helping on my arms and legs), it also gave me some dramatic dark circles under my eyes. Even as a child I looked as if I needed about two weeks of deep sleep. Needless to say, I've become an expert on concealing those rings around my eyes. A matte concealer will stay on longer, but make sure to use a lightweight undereye moisturizer instead of a heavy cream, or the concealer will slide off and you'll look like a Salvador Dalí painting.

My mother-in-law swore by Nivea products, and over the years she convinced me. She used the heaviest Nivea cream under her eyes every single night and morning. When she was in her late seventies she had fewer crow's feet than an actual crow. My theory is that Nivea is so heavy you can't move your eyes enough to create a wrinkle.

I can't tell you how many times I read in women's magazines about putting cucumber slices on the eyes. It usually involved taking a half hour before that all-important dinner party to put your feet up and relax while the cukes did their stuff. As if I ever had any spare time for myself when putting on a shindig! Frankly, I thought it was a bunch of hooey. But one afternoon when I was completely frazzled after spending two hours talking a teenage daughter out of a nose ring, I tried it. The chilled veggies felt great on my eyes. I kept them on until they had warmed to room temperature. When I opened my eyes I thought I'd done something wrong because the juices from the cukes covered my eyeballs and my vision was blurry. I was pretty certain I'd blinded myself. Bravely, I blinked. Wow! My vision cleared, and when I looked in the mirror my eyes looked terrific. Vegetables really are good for you!

You Are What You Eat

And that little anecdote, ladies, brings us to food. Funny how that keeps coming up, isn't it? We all know that certain foods can directly convert to saddle-bags and spare tires and our faces aren't immune to a poor diet either. If you subsist on doughnuts, French fries, and chocolate, your skin will pay the price by appearing flaccid, sallow, and blemished. If that doesn't scare you away from the drive-through, you may be beyond help.

Come on, eat your vegetables—and fruits and whole grains. While I have no scientific proof to back up my theory, I feel that the effects of a side dish of Brussels sprouts with dinner has a positive effect on the skin that is visible when you look in the mirror the next morning. I must admit to some mixed feelings about this much-maligned (and often by me) vegetable. It's kind of like men—they don't always smell so great and they're a bit gassy, but once they've had a chance to work on your body you can see a whole new glow.

And don't forget lots of water to hydrate your skin from the inside out. The benefits of drinking water include the promotion of regular elimination of waste and toxins and—miracle of miracles—it's also a real key to keeping your weight down.

Think of your skin as a flower, and give it the nutrients and care it craves.

Roll Over and Perk Up

Now, this may sound weird, but when I was a young woman I noticed how older women had wrinkles on the chest between their breasts. I decided that it wouldn't happen to me and so I actually trained myself to sleep on my back! It worked, and over time I realized that I had also done my face a favor. If you habitually sleep on one side, you'll notice that those "marionette" lines around your mouth are deeper on that side. These days you can buy any number of special neck pillows—foam, flax, buckwheat, or oddball miracle fiber—that will keep your head and neck sufficiently elevated and straight to both prevent your face from getting smushed and keep your boobs a respectable distance from each other.

Be Consistent

There is one rule I never break. No matter how tired or sick I am, or even if I've had too much to drink, I never, ever go to bed without washing my face. And believe me, there have been plenty of times I've been lucky to be able to *find* the bathroom sink, much less go through some complicated cleansing process. But for me, the great motivator is not waking up with raccoon eyes and brackish smudges on my pillowcase. I'm sure that image works for you, too.

More importantly, the makeup will clog your pores and cause lines and blemishes, but you probably already know that, even if you weren't paying attention to your mother. Heaven knows I've tried to pass the knowledge on to my own daughters, but they are about as receptive as a pair of Sphinxes. Most days I feel lucky just to talk them out of wearing black lipstick.

Shall We Dance?

Even if you've never danced, give it a try

*Nobody cares if you can't dance well.
Just get up and dance. Great dancers are not
great because of their technique,
they are great because of their passion.*

—MARTHA GRAHAM

*I*f you've never learned to dance, it's about time to do so. If you already know how, it's time to brush up on your skills, both technical and social. It's a great way to meet new people and, depending upon the style of dance you choose, you just might get a good workout to boot.

When my marriage broke up, my children lived with me every other week. Dancing saved my life during the weeks they were gone. It not only soothed the loneliness, but I was so exhausted after a night on my feet that I fell asleep the moment I hit the sheets. Of course, five hours of nonstop exercise can take quite a toll, especially in the beginning. I remember how much my feet hurt when I came home that first night, but also how much my face glowed the next morning.

There's something quite magical about dancing. You probably know that by watching it, but you may not yet have succumbed to the seduction of its performance. By performance, I don't mean to say that you are under some obligation to put on a show. I'm talking about the actual feeling of the steps and routines that allow you to surrender your body to the music. Once you do that, all other concerns evaporate. Music, it's well known, is therapeutic. Soothes the savage breast and all that.

Everyone Can Dance

Don't know any smooth moves? Well, not all dances are complicated. I chose to learn a dance called West Coast Swing, partly because I like the music. It's a lot like the music our generation grew up with—a good sensual beat, lyrics to die for, and a rhythm and blues flavor. It's easy to move to even if you don't have the precise steps down.

Those who danced were thought to be quite in-sane by those who could not hear the music.

— ANGELA MONET

A good teacher is a blessing, but here's a tip that will save you many hours of lesson time: Most dances are a combination of doubles (walking steps) and triples (right-left-right or left-right-left). If you can master those simple combos you are ready to learn any dance. And you can rent any number of instructional videos for virtually any dance. These sometimes help get you over those first-night jitters in a lesson situation.

Even if you don't have a partner, there are still plenty of occasions for a single woman to dance. Country western dancing is possibly the most easygoing situation for the solo female. Even women who come with partners are free to circulate and dance with others, if only to experience some different styles. And, of course, there is always the option of line dancing, which doesn't require a partner, just a little bit of memorization. Anytime somebody puts together a few cool moves on the dance floor it's an excuse to make up a line and get scootin'.

Join in the fun and maybe you'll meet the dance mate of a lifetime.

Going to adult dance events is usually a good social opportunity. People who dance for hobby or sport are usually there purely for the love of dancing and are not just on the make. It's always possible, of course, that you might meet the man of your dreams (and how dreamy it would be to have one that can dance!), but even setting that expectation aside, what a fabulous and exhilarating feeling it is to be *in* the music and glide in sync with a partner. Oh, and keep your eye on that short guy—he's usually a better dancer than the tall one. And if he can dance well, there's a distinct possibility that he's probably also good in bed. At least you know he's got rhythm.

Tried and True

If you're looking to find a dancing comfort zone, you might want to try the Arthur Murray Studios. There's one in just about every major city, not just in the United States, but all around the world. It starts with an introductory evaluation so that you wind up in classes with people of like ability. This is a great place to learn a variety of dances, which can serve you well socially. The older woman who knows The Ropes knows she'll look more elegant doing the samba than flailing around the floor dancing freestyle.

The foxtrot is a simple dance that fits a lot of different tempos, and if you can do the foxtrot you can definitely waltz. Oh, how I love a man who can waltz! The tango is a bit more complicated, but you can master it with a few extra lessons. It's best to take tango lessons with a prearranged partner because there are so many different styles. It helps if you both know what the other is doing.

There's one more dance craze that's sweeping across the bedrooms of America—pole dancing. Yes, that's what strippers do. You don't have to wear a G-string to do it, although if you think you can pull it off, by all means go for it! Believe me, the moves are sexy enough to be effective on your male companion even if you were wearing galoshes and a peacoat. You can sign up for a series of lessons for a couple of hundred dollars. Then all you need is a portable pole, which you can buy at Home Depot. Even if there's no man in your life, this is great exercise for toning the glutes, thighs, arms, and abs. The music is your choice, of course, as is the lucky benefactor of your newly acquired and provocative expertise.

There are Arthur Murray Studios in ten countries around the world, including Japan, South Africa, and Egypt. So you have no excuse—get out there and dance.

Best of all, the Arthur Murray Studios have dance parties every week right there in the studio. It's not a bar scene and you can feel comfortable going there alone. You'll already know some of the people and all of them will have learned more or less the same steps and techniques that you have learned.

When you're first learning to dance with a partner, you might want to try counting in your head (1, 2, cha cha cha) so you can stay on the beat no matter what moves your partner leads. When you're making turns, keep counting and continue to do the steps throughout the turn. You'll end up in the right place and on the right foot and your partner will think you dance like a pro!

It's Not Just the Dance

There are more benefits to be gained from hitting the dance floor than just socializing. About a half hour of dancing is all you need to burn off that extra muffin you shouldn't have eaten at breakfast, so if you dance all night—well, you do the math. And a spirited twenty minutes of salsa dancing is a much more satisfying way to get that all-important cardio workout than watching soaps as you plod along on the treadmill. There's also a magical thing that seems to keep you from sweating when you're in a little black dress and twirling across the floor.

> *Remember, Ginger Rogers did everything Fred Astaire did, but she did it backward and in high heels.*

Personally, I like the tradition of dressing up to go dancing. Not only do I feel better about myself, I also believe it is a gesture of respect to your partner(s). I'm sure it's appreciated when a woman brings a little glamour to the dance floor. Besides, the more attractive the flower, the more bees are likely to buzz around.

It's mandatory to smell your best, but don't put it on with a ladle. You don't want your scent to stay on the man after the dance is over. I know I hate it when a man's cologne is so heavy I want to call the aroma police. A hint of aftershave and a good clean smell is so much more appealing. Cosmetic commercials have erroneously convinced women that their scent should precede their actual presence in a room, like some sort of olfactory warning sign. I say a man should be given the privilege of getting close to you before he gets to know what you smell like.

For glamour, there's nothing like salsa dancing, which is all the rage these days. Ruffled skirts, high strappy heels, perhaps a fresh flower in your hair (I grow gardenias in my garden so I can pluck one to tuck behind my ear just before I go dancing).

One wants to make sure the view is appealing when making those sharp rapid spins, so whatever you choose to put under that skirt, make sure your butt is covered. Literally. Thigh-high stockings are out of the loop, as well as thong underwear. Save those for dancing in your bedroom.

Ah, dancing in the bedroom! Let's talk about that right now. If you are just too shy or inhibited to do your thing in public, dancing in the privacy of your own bedroom is certainly the best alternative. It's the perfect place to let your inner tiger out. And, darlings, this means with or without male company. Put on some music, find the beat, and let it move your body in any way that feels natural to you; just go ahead and be the dancing goddess you know you are.

Do it in front of the mirror, do it naked, do it in the dark, but do it!

Going for Glamour

The older woman can use dramatic flair

> *Any girl can be glamorous. All you have to do*
> *is stand still and look stupid.*
>
> —HEDY LAMARR

One of the most important ways in which we declare our identity, especially as we get older, is how we dress and present ourselves. We can look conservative in business suits, we can adopt the old "screw beauty" attitude by getting a crew cut and wearing workout clothes as a uniform, or we can go the glamorous route. I always opt for glamour. Some women are immediately intimidated by the very word. Let's get over that right now. After all, what is glamour?

In order to be irreplaceable one must always be different.

— COCO CHANEL

To begin with, you don't have to be beautiful—or even pretty, for that matter—to be glamorous. It's all about style and savoir faire. According to the dictionary, glamour is "alluring charm, fascinating attractiveness." Notice it does not say "pretty," does not say "young," does not say "beautiful." So that would be a "go" for all of us, right?

Let's break it down. Alluring charm—your particular charm, that which draws people to you. It is that certain something that is unique to your personality and how you convey it. Whether it's the scarf you drape over your shoulder, your wholesomeness, your self-confidence, your openness, or your general style. It doesn't mean that you shouldn't go for a bit of drama (because we can pull it off at our age), it just means that you needn't force the issue. Just learn to be comfortable in asserting who you are and how much you have to offer. Own that, and you will own the world. Or at least a corner of it, preferably the corner with the handsome gentleman holding the door for you (see "Hello, He Lied").

Charm is difficult to define clearly. The author Albert Camus said it is a way of getting the answer yes without asking a question. It is also the art of making other people feel at ease, no matter the situation. Some people can transform an awkward social moment into a round of relieved laughter with just one charming remark. Strive to be one of those people, one who always makes others feel as if *they* are the interesting party.

You can even be a little bit mysterious. You needn't start out every new social opportunity by telling everyone how fabulous you are (and certainly not how badly things have been going for you), or even very much at all about who you are. In this particular arena, silence is golden. Your demeanor will tell others you are special and they will want to know you. And when they finally drag information out of you, be truthful, but brief. And as soon as possible, divert the conversation back to the questioners by asking them about themselves. That will make them not only want to know more, but will gain you a reputation as a charming conversationalist, for your conversation dwells upon others rather than yourself. A good listener ends up being the keeper of secrets and confidences, not to mention the receiver of the occasional good stock tip.

What Is Attractive?

As for the attractiveness part, it's ridiculously easy. Attractive is nearly synonymous with neat. Keep it neat and simple. Good grooming makes anyone more attractive to be sure. Put yourself together every single day and not because you have plans to see someone special that day. Do it for yourself. You are, after all, the person you spend the most time with and you ought to at least give yourself something nice to look at. Anybody else who happens to be around can only benefit from feasting their eyes upon you. Again, you don't have to be drop-dead gorgeous; you just have to learn how to display your best assets at all times. It's not necessary to be dressed up and made up at all times, but you don't want someone to run into you on the street and mistake you for a bag lady. Although I must say I've seen some shopping-cart ladies who have quite a bit of style and even attempt to add their own touch of glamour with a feather boa or a rakish fedora.

And speaking of hats, now is the time for you to wear them with aplomb. Nothing adds to winter glamour like a cashmere beret or a smart wool cloche—and you'll be toasty warm as well. And hats are a great way to frame your perfectly made-up eyes and lips, not to mention a camouflage trick for those less-than-perfect hair days. And a good hat will last you decades. Most winter hats never really go out of fashion—just be sure to avoid those with plaid earflaps.

Summer hat styles change a bit more frequently, especially with the younger set. Just avoid anything seen on a teen pop star and proceed from there. A good straw hat, especially a Panama, not only provides crucial shelter from the sun, but a beautiful summer or spring look. Unless you're one of those lucky women who can wear a fisherman's hat and magically make it look glamorous, just stick with the classics.

I'm not suggesting that you emulate the downtrodden, but I cannot stress enough that glamour doesn't have to be expensive. It just requires a little thought and ingenuity. You can do wonders with a black turtleneck and a big scarf or a long string of pearls. Use your accessories sparingly so that they are striking additions rather than a collection of Christmas tree ornaments.

By all means, be inventive. My mother gave me all her old handkerchiefs—embroidered, tatted, lace-trimmed, and monogrammed. To me, they were treasures, and I couldn't see blowing my nose on them, so I started tying them around my wrist. I was wearing one of the hankies one night while having dinner with a friend (who tells this story with relish). She cooed and carried on as if I had just invented the wheel. A week or so later, she called me to say that she had started wearing handkerchiefs around her wrists because she just couldn't get over how chic and inventive it was. But, she said, everyone thought she was wearing a bandage and speculation had begun that perhaps she had become so depressed that she had attempted suicide. And so, you see, one woman's chic is another woman's faux pas.

Everyday Glamour

It's crucial to give yourself criteria for how you will allow yourself to be seen in public. Personally, I absolutely will not step out of my house without mascara, lipstick, and a little blush. It takes only a moment, but for me it makes all the difference in how I feel as well as how I look.

I never go out unless I look like Joan Crawford the movie star. If you want to see the girl next door, go next door.

— JOAN CRAWFORD

More importantly, I won't go outside dressed like a lazy teenager (is there any other kind?). To be sure, tennis shoes and sweats have their place in life, but if the gym isn't included in the trip, don't dress like a frump. Let's face it, have you ever really looked at your butt in sweats? This is not a flattering look on an older woman. In fact, it doesn't look all that good on a woman of any age. Besides, the very word "sweats" implies that you're going to do just that. If you're going to sweat, heaven forbid, make sure it's while doing something really fun—and preferably with a partner!

In the clothing department, glamour isn't about sequins and flash. It's not what you're wearing as much as it is *how* you're wearing it. I saw a woman try on a plainly cut ivory-colored wool jacket and discard it because it looked, well, boring. Another woman snatched it off the rack and slipped it on. For a moment it looked just as plain as it had on the first woman, and then she pushed up the sleeves, turned up the collar, and voilà! Glamorous! The first woman looked confused, disappointed, and perhaps even a tiny bit bitter. She was probably wondering why she didn't look that good in the jacket. Ah, well, style is a big part of glamour. As the saying goes, class is something one is born into, style is something one acquires.

You'd be surprised how much it costs to look this cheap.

— DOLLY PARTON

Fascinating You

Now I suppose you're wondering how to be fascinating. Again, it's in the definition of the word. It means to inspire great interest and attraction. There you go, darlings. If you look fabulous and you know it, you'll exude confidence and everyone is going to be drawn to you.

And of course they'll be interested, because they're going to be wondering how in the world you pull it off! It doesn't hurt to be up on current events beyond the world of fashion. It doesn't take much time to read the newspaper every day (and if you do it on the stationary bike, you'll look better, too) so that you can keep up with the conversation. It's not just about the news, either. Try to find out more about a subject that intrigues you every week—read a book about unusual inventions or research endangered species online. Whatever it takes to keep your mind active and give you more options. And of course, be a good listener. You needn't hold court to be fascinating. You need only to provide the flame to attract those moths, er, admirers.

Everyone has an invisible sign hanging from his neck saying, "Make me feel important."

When it comes down to it, glamour is about the willingness to be different. Not a sheep, but an individual. It's a form of bravery, really. It says, "I'm not afraid to show a little attitude, a flair, perhaps even a little innovation. I'm still alive, still creative, still proud of myself, and still appreciating beauty wherever I find it." And the best place to find it is within yourself.

The pundits now say that sixty is the new fifty. Well, being fit, chic, and youthful is the new glamour, no matter what your age!

Live and Let Diet

Going for a slimmer you

> *I've been on a diet for two weeks and all I've lost is two weeks.*
>
> —TOTIE FIELDS

*W*omen always seem to struggle with food. What to eat? When? How much? Well, one thing is as clear as bouillon: You should not, and *cannot* eat as much as you once did. Eating smaller portions of everything is crucial.

We've all fallen prey to weird diets, to be sure, especially when we were younger. But by now we've all learned that there is no joy in a week of eating grapefruit and hardboiled eggs or trying to sustain life on cabbage soup. Let the wisdom of age prevail when it comes to your waistline.

Brussels sprouts are only sixty calories per cup, but who cares?

While I would never go so far as to recommend a diet to anyone, I can certainly tell you how I keep myself a size six. After trying just about everything, I've discovered what works for me, and it's food combining, which was originally derived from the well-known experiments that Pavlov performed on his dogs. Pavlov's work with dogs showed that starches are digested in about two hours, and proteins are digested in about four hours; but a protein/starch mixture can still be digesting thirteen hours later, and food taken on top of this mixture can lead to fermentation and toxic by-products, putting strain on the system. All this information was put together by Dr. William Howard Hay in 1911, and although everyone made fun of him, the idea held on through the decades to become one of the most popular diet theories.

There are lots of books on food combining, but I have found Suzanne Somers's books to be the most accessible. She has several books describing the theory along with some simple but delicious recipes. The results are dramatic, and the best part is that I never feel deprived of anything. At my age, I have absolutely no interest in deprivation of any kind.

—————————————————————————————————

Life itself is the proper binge.

— JULIA CHILD

And here's a real bonus: On the food-combining program you'll never have gas. Now, girls, let's face it, gas is one of the more unpleasant, not to mention embarrassing, quirks of the older body. God has such a peculiar sense of humor, does she not? We already had to suffer with bleeding, bloating, and cramps through adolescence and adulthood, endured the wrenching pain of childbirth, and then the final insult of menopause and its accompanying hot flashes, night sweats, and mood swings. Just when we think we have finally paid our dues we get hit with unscheduled and uncontrolled flatulence. If only we could figure out a way to harness this gas power, the world's fuel shortage would be over.

The simplified version of the food-combining technique is merely to avoid eating proteins and carbohydrates at the same meal. In fact, one should put three or four hours in between the consumption of, say, a

sirloin steak and the baked potato that would ordinarily accompany it. Milk and cereal are no longer best
friends. Of course, there are always those days when
the chili dog (which involves both carbs and protein
along with an ample serving of fat) becomes somehow
irresistible, so make sure you have some gas relief
tablets tucked away in your handbag for just such
windy emergencies.

Different Strokes

I have a dear friend, also a size six, who approaches her
dieting in a different way. She's very physically active
and starts every morning with a soft-boiled egg and a
piece of steak or a sausage patty. Then she's off to the
gym before starting the rest of her day. She pretty
much stays with all protein through lunch, so that by
dinnertime she can blow her carbs all at once, usually
on wine and pasta. In addition, she counts calories religiously. She knows the calorie count for every food item
known to womankind, from peanuts to foie gras, and
computes what she's going to eat and drink by how
many calories she's expended during her morning
workout. "A half hour on the StairMaster and I've
earned myself a few free beers," she reasons. By keeping

her caloric intake at about 1,400, she never has an extra pound to deal with. Her dessert of choice is diet Jell-O with fresh raspberries and fake whipped topping—thirty-five calories. "Violent physical exercise is the key," she says, "and after that you can do whatever the hell you want." If you live.

> It'll take you two hours to walk off the 960 calories in a cup of macadamia nuts, but you'll burn off all the calories in a stalk of celery just by eating it.

Here's another quick fix if you're only a few pounds overweight: a diet shake like Slim-Fast for breakfast, berries as a midmorning snack, a frozen diet meal for lunch, an afternoon fruit snack, and another diet meal for dinner. Do this for five days and you'll lose a few pounds, just enough to loosen that waistband. And think of how much money you'll save! After all, one of those skinny frozen dinners is only a couple of bucks, while it's hard to get out of even a fast-food restaurant for less than five dollars, not to mention hundreds of calories.

Good eating habits go a long way toward maintaining both your weight and, more importantly, your health. A couple of simple practices can get you on the right road. First, avoid refined sugar. It turns directly into fat without even passing "go."

The second vital habit to take up is drinking lots of water. Lots and lots of water; I mean it. It sounds so simple, but it really does help flush out the body's toxins and keep the weight off. Unless, of course, you're using your water to chase down chocolate éclairs.

No matter what sort of diet you choose, you might want to brush up on your calorie counting so you'll be aware of silly pitfalls. The most innocent-looking things (like olives, for instance) can pack a wallop. Interestingly, the more expensive or rare the food, it seems the more likely it is to be lower in calories. Caviar is only about 30 calories per tablespoon; blueberries are practically a free ride, and they have the added bonus of being an antioxidant. Of course, you'll have a whopper of a grocery bill, but at least you won't have to shell out a fortune for a new supersized wardrobe.

Older, Wiser, Chubbier

Even if you're one of those people who has never had a weight problem (bitch!), you may find yourself with a few extra pounds when you get to the second half of your life. But that's where the wisdom of age comes in: You can figure out how to nip this potential chubbiness in the bud.

A 125-pound woman needs around 1,650 calories to maintain her weight at the age of thirty. By forty she needs 1,600, but when she turns fifty she'll need only about 1,540 . . . and so on and so on. . . .

The number of calories you need to maintain your perfect weight decreases by 2 to 4 percent every decade, so it really is true that you can't eat the same things you did when you were young. Not that you'd want to still be subsisting on burgers, fries, and shakes. You'd be paying that bill with cellulite, for heaven's sake. Besides, a double Whopper with cheese checks in at a whopping 1,010 calories, although without mayo it's only 820. And those fancy coffee drinks like a Frappuccino are almost 500 calories, so if you need your caffeine fix, try just eating a few chocolate-covered espresso beans. Go with dark chocolate, as it helps suppress the appetite. Yeah, and it releases those endorphins that make you feel rather as if you are in love, only without the heartbreak. Unless you eat too much of it, and then you're just breaking your own heart, along with your diet.

Save 100 calories by holding the mayo on your sandwich.

Personally, I can't bring myself to eat diet Jell-O, or anything resembling it, for dessert. I long for the real deal, and I'm a pushover for a cannoli, but I do have a trick. When it comes to the old-fashioned, rich, delicious, calorie-laden desserts that I crave, I make do with a few bites. I get the sweet rush and the sensual pleasure without doing any real damage or giving myself a case of guilt. I find it helpful to take myself on a mental time-travel voyage back to first grade when I discovered that flour and water mixed together make *paste*. Try visualizing that when you are poised to wolf down the paste-try.

Innovative Weight-Control Techniques

Okay, so you hate to diet and you hate to exercise even more. With a little creativity you may yet be able to expend those calories without getting near a gym. Next time your man gets the hots for you, insist upon being on top. That's about 300 more calories than the missionary position. And if you can do it while hanging from the crystal chandelier, you can consider yourself ahead by 1,000 calories. And once you get going, don't even bother to try for a real orgasm because that's only about 100 calories; but if you fake it with gusto, you could burn as much as 315!

Or you could go bowling. Three hours of knocking down pins and you'll earn yourself a small bag of French fries. It's all in how you do the math.

gardening: 350 cal/hour, softball: 150 cal/hour, swimming: 500 cal/hour, golf: 225 cal/hour, slow dancing: 125 cal/hour

New Uses for Your Mouth

Finally, there is one tried-and-true tummy trimmer: Don't eat after 6:00 P.M. It's an old model's trick, and it works like a charm. It stands to reason that if nothing passes your lips, you won't be gaining any weight. It's not that easy, though, especially if you're one of those midnight snackers. You'll just have to figure out something else to do with your mouth and hands in the evening. Either learn to crochet and chew sugarless gum or read the "Romance in the Dark" chapter and try to figure out what new purpose you might find for those lovely lips.

I recommend the latter. It's bound to be more fun.

Size Doesn't Matter

Don't let your dress size get in the way of your style

> *Can you imagine a world without men?*
> *No crime and lots of happy fat women.*
> —SYLVIA (NICOLE HOLLANDER)

I'm fat! I don't look like those people in the fashion magazines. If I could only get my thighs down to twig size, if I could only have a smaller butt, if I could only. . . .

Oh, get over it! No one looks like that, not even the models. There's a world of airbrushing and sleight of hand that goes on to make those babes look like, well, babes. Take heart, you needn't be an anorexic vixen to be sexy. Unlike diamonds and men, with women, size really is not important.

Seventy-six out of a hundred men say they prefer a woman with a bit of meat on her bones.

Most of all, remember that not every man desires a woman so thin he might cut himself to shreds when he rolls over onto her in the middle of the night. I am reminded of the time I attended a beach party in Hawaii that was hosted by a pair of local singers, Frankie and Johnny. Frankie was the huge Samoan who greeted us. I was on some trendy diet and was proud of my 115-pound slenderness and how flat my stomach was in my hip-hugger skirt.

Frankie looked me up and down in what I thought was a flattering assessment of my svelte figure. Then he turned to my date and said with an air of genuine curiosity, "So, you like a *skinny* woman, huh? Myself, I like a waterbed." With that, he gestured toward the fulsome Johnny who, decked out in an almost totally concealing but brightly colored sarong, was surrounded by adoring men. Frankie looked proud of Johnny, and I felt like a stringy chicken for the rest of the night. Everyone had considerable tummies except for me. Moreover, nobody gave me a second glance.

Hey, have you ever really looked at Marilyn Monroe's body? She was, although personal accounts and urban legends differ, somewhere between a size twelve and a fourteen. She had a little belly, and that layer of fat probably improved her bustline dramatically. Remember, this was before the age of implants. Today she might be obsessed with getting skinny. Can you picture Marilyn's face on a rail-thin Calista Flockhart body?

Twelve Is the New Two

Let's face it, not everyone is a size six, or even an eight or a ten. And the way size varies in clothing these days, who knows what size you really are? In some clothing lines the old-school twelve is a two, and those skinny girls actually get to say they're wearing a zero! And that's why I say that size is not important. It's all in how you use it and how you display it (or hide it). Style is the essence of your presentation, not size. Get comfortable in your skin and know that you are a gorgeous woman.

We all know the rules about no horizontal stripes and no intense floral patterns. It doesn't take a fashion genius to figure out that stuff makes you look fat. But there are slimming tricks you may not have thought of, many of which are employed by television, movie, and rock stars.

If your hips are your problem, try to avoid the Shania Twain/Janet Jackson long flared-coat look. It only makes it more obvious. Instead, go for a long, slender drape over a straight-line shift. If you have great legs, let them dangle out, or if you think your calves are too fat, find some soft boots that aren't totally formfitting. Bring the attention upward toward your fabulous face, and know that if a man isn't looking in your eyes to begin with, he's the wrong guy.

In 2004, the average American woman weighed about 160 pounds.

If your upper body is thick, you more than likely have cleavage that's the envy of your Skinny Minnie friends. Go ahead and show it off, but not in the form of a tight-fitting bodice. You want to be a role model, not a "roll" model. Dolman sleeves will camouflage your upper arms, and you can go with a slender cuff if your wrists aren't too pudgy. You can cover a multitude of sins with a loose-fitting top and long, flowing sleeves. Just make certain it's not too sheer, or you'll defeat the purpose.

The range of clothing lines for the plus-size woman is truly amazing. You don't have to settle for dumpy muumuus or tent dresses anymore. Liz Claiborne, Delta Burke, and many others have created elegant clothing lines for the large and lovely, and Queen Latifah has done wonders for supersized lingerie in her role as a Lane Bryant model. Ralph Lauren, Ellen Tracy, and Eileen Fisher are just a few of the designers who have wised up and created clothing that won't feel skimpy around the thighs and arms. And there are department stores like Saks that have whole floors devoted to you.

Fashion is architecture. It's a matter of proportions.

— COCO CHANEL

Another size issue for women is height. If you're over six feet tall, you might wear up to a size fourteen, but standard sizes will look all wrong on your frame. Rather than go with an endless parade of shirt dresses, go online to look up a company called Design Elevations (DesignElevations.com) to find designer fashions for women up to six feet, six inches.

If you're a catalogue kind of girl (I love them— from Lands' End to Neiman Marcus), you can shop at your own pace and experiment with sizing and styles. The well-known catalogues have great return services and save you time, money, and the discouragement in the shopping process. If you order a number of things at once, the shipping is much lower per item and you can have your own little shopping spree at home. If you haven't shopped with a particular catalogue before, it's a good idea to give them a jingle (yes, the old-fashioned telephone) and find out how their sizing chart works. Again, sizes vary widely, so get specific measurements and match them up to your own. That way, at least you'll be in the ballpark of your own size. After a while you'll get to know what size to order from what catalogue.

Consider the plus-size model. She's between a size twelve and a sixteen. She's robust, confident, and most of all, she's realistic.

You can use the Internet to find online catalogues and shopping services. Some shopping sites feature quality photos of the clothing from different angles. You'll be astounded at the range of styles and prices. Oh, and don't forget eBay for great bargains on designer stuff.

Or, if you want to go more hands-on when looking for great designer stuff, start haunting the upscale resale shops. You needn't forgo fabulous beaded ball gowns or Chanel suits just because you don't look like a celery stick. Wealthy women come in large sizes as well, and often there are some fabulous bargains to be had because the bigger sizes don't sell as quickly. Also, don't be afraid to try on something that you think is a size too small, because ofttimes higher-priced clothing is sized more generously, as if paying more entitles you to be a size six instead of a ten. Just hold it up and see if you've got a prayer, then try it on! I once bought a former Nancy Reagan gown that was pretending to be a three and it fit my size-six bod like a glove! The dyed-to-match Givenchy shoes were total gunboats, but I bought them anyway and put cotton in the toes to make them fit.

Make no mistake, this is not to say that you shouldn't watch your weight and be diligent about exercise. It's just that you needn't try to make your body conform to some mythical, media-propelled proportions that very few of us can attain. Before you opt for liposuction or body sculpting, try to see what clothing can do for you, not what you can do for your clothing.

There is some evidence that the emaciated look is on the way out. Young girls who favor low-rise jeans (and don't *you* dare be seen with your waistband just above your pubic hair) are now sporting little rolls of baby fat near the belly button piercing. For one thing, it's easier to pierce something if you can actually get a grip on it, and it's probably a whole lot more comfortable to wear a belly ring if you have a little bit of belly, fondly referred to by these fulsome creatures as "the pouch."

While this doesn't mean you should let yourself go completely to pot (belly) and start studding yourself with rings and nails, it does give us all a little bit of hope that the American ideal of the female body is moving to something softer and more realistic. And you have to be realistic about your own body. You need to take off excess weight if only for your health, but you should be sensible about it. Meanwhile, you can still look your best, whatever your weight.

Besides, you know how someone always points out that the sexiest part of your body is your brain? Well, you should know that the brain is made up entirely of fat. So if you got rid of all the fat in your body, your brain would disappear and then you'd have to run for public office. Think about how *that* would mess up your life.

The upshot is this, girls: No matter what size you are, you've got it. We've all got it. Sometimes we just have to remember how to use it.

Fashionista!

Taking a good look at your wardrobe

> *I base most of my fashion taste on
> what doesn't itch.*
> —GILDA RADNER

The most important thing to learn about fashion is objectivity. You need to know the absolute truth about how you look in what you're wearing. You certainly can't count on the salesperson, for he or she would tell you that you look terrific in a plastic garbage bag with beaded fringe if it meant a hefty sale. I shudder when I see a fiftyish woman decked out in a dog collar and a leather miniskirt that barely covers her cellulite, looking like she's on her way to a techno rave. I always wonder just what kind of evil spirit was in the dressing room with her, whispering,

"You look *wonderful* in that!" It couldn't have been a friend, even if she always said she was.

Do you have a real friend that always looks smashing? She's the one you want to invite with you when you go shopping. She'll know just the right words to say when you've tried on a sleeveless something that shows off the flab on your upper arms that you've managed to ignore for months or years. That's when a true friend will use code. "You know how cold you get at night, darling," she'll coo. "Perhaps you should go for something with sleeves." What she means, of course, is, "If you are seen on the street in that, I'll pretend I don't know you."

Does fashion matter? Always—though not quite so much after death.

— JOAN RIVERS

There's a time to recognize when the skirt is too short, the neckline too plunging, the waistline too tight. Once you're in your late forties you need to let go of cute and run screaming from trendy. It's time to discover what works for you. This is when you must start to avoid "mother of the bride" fabrics like chiffon. Even if you *are* the mother of the bride.

As much as I hated it, I gave up shorts—at least in public—in my fifties. Even one little varicose vein is an incredible turnoff. I know, I know . . . you love your short shorts. It's hard, but unless you are one of those lucky women who still possesses silky smooth, unblemished legs, exchange those shorts for something longer like toreador pants. And please don't be one of those desperate creatures who tries to get around the issue by wearing panty hose under shorts. It makes the legs look like a pair of sausages about to burst from their casings.

Twisted Tootsies

Other things that often must go by the wayside as we grow older are sandals and open-toed shoes. Once the feet have logged forty or so years in high heels, the toes show the mileage. Unless your little piggies are totally corn-free and flat, cover them. And if you have bunions, I can tell you without fear of contradiction that nobody wants to see them.

This doesn't mean that you have to live your life in clodhoppers or ankle boots even in the peak of summer.

Sling-back pumps or flats are a wonderful alternative to thongs or sandals, but make sure you take a good look at your heels. If despite your best efforts they are still dry and cracked, cover them. Don't worry, there are plenty of attractive alternatives that will keep you stylish and fend off wisecracks about your feet looking like claws—the sort of innocent remark you are likely to hear from little children, who are much closer to the floor.

If you like wearing trousers, choose comfortable loafers, flats, driving moccasins, or even sneakers (clean, color-coordinated, and stylish, of course). Personally, I find the look of pants or jeans with a leather or suede car shoe stunningly chic. And a black-and-white pin-striped pantsuit with gleaming white tennies is so gangsta hip!

I still like the look of heels, but I've put the really high ones away except for special occasions. I never like to see an older woman teetering about on stiletto heels. The words "hip fracture" immediately leap to mind.

Graduate to Glamour

Just because you're no spring chicken doesn't mean that you have to look like an old biddy. Your maturity gives you license to go for drama and glamour. Now you can pull back your hair in a chignon, turn up your collar, and sweep into the room in a long, dramatic coat. Think Lauren Bacall. The turtleneck (or a good plastic surgeon) becomes your best friend after a certain age. Strategically placed scarves can make a world of difference, too.

A pair of kid gloves are lovely with a winter coat, but unless you're Diane Keaton, it's unlikely you can pull off gloves with a summer dress and a man's hat and necktie. That's hard enough to do when you're in your twenties, and as you get older this is the kind of style no-no that can get you mistaken for a lunatic.

Also, no more Stevie Nicks gypsy getups after fifty—you know, platform boots and flowing scarves with beaded fringe. Leave those kinds of kinky fashion statements to the younger set. In short, avoid any look that is contrived or eccentric and strive for the simple, classic, and slightly tailored.

Unburn That Bra

Were you one of those hippie children who ran joyously through the fields of wildflowers (well, figuratively, anyway), free and unfettered by a brassiere? Did you ceremoniously burn that uncomfortable binding garment in a public ceremony? It might be time to reconsider. Even I, who can still pass "the pencil test" (firm enough breasts that a pencil cannot be snugly tucked beneath one of them), have recently acquired quite a wardrobe of bras. I made the decision after I caught my reflection in a store window. Yikes! Could those be my beautiful tits drifting downward toward my shoes? I now pass on tops that require one to go braless.

Of course, you don't want to *look* like you're wearing a bra, and there are some wonderfully innovative and deceptive booby traps on the market these days. Off the shoulder, shelf, backless, magnetic, the choices are endless. Just make sure that you go to a proper lingerie shop and definitely avoid anything that's advertised on television. Buy a Chia Pet or a roll-up flathose if you must, but resist the temptation to buy some sort of "miracle bra" that you've not actually tried on.

There is one of those miracle contraptions that actually does work. It's two bra cups made of that kind of weird rubbery goo that your children used to love—the stuff that slithered down the wall. Well, it's not quite that bad, but at first it's a little weird. You plaster these flesh colored cups on your boobs (sticky side in, of course) and then attach them together with a little plastic clasp. Voilà! Instant lift and cleavage. No kidding, these babies really work. It's not meant to replace your regular bra, but for those special backless evenings or garden parties, this is a marvelous invention. The most popular one is called the NuBra, and it can be found in high-end lingerie shops. I know one adventurous soul who even wore hers under her bathing suit while body-surfing in Hawaii and it stayed firmly attached.

Fashionista Wardrobe Makeover

Rethinking and redoing your wardrobe doesn't necessarily take a lot of money. If you're on a budget (and who isn't?), try a shop that specializes in used designer duds. If there isn't a used designer clothing outlet near you, you might consider going to eBay for some great bargains. With a bit of diligence, you can find elegant, high-fashion outfits that are barely worn or even never worn. If you aren't sure what size you take in designer wear (which can be very different than department store stuff), be sure to ask the seller a lot of specific questions about measurements. Then, of course, be honest with yourself about your own measurements before you shell out your hard-earned money (even alimony is earned, darlings).

While it's great fun to experiment with a host of different looks as a girl, a grown-up woman should have her own style. If you haven't done it yet, it's time for a little R&D (research and development). First, pick out your very favorite outfits from your own closet—a few things you look really smashing in. Study the silhouettes and determine what basic styles suit you. These are things you must find more of.

It is chic not to be too chic.

— ELSIE DE WOLFE

Then, what color brings out your eyes, your skin, your hair? Be careful here: Although hot pink or lime green may suit your skin tone, it doesn't necessarily mean that you have to deck yourself out like a Christmas tree. But splashes of color are wonderful, even if you look great in basic black.

Whenever possible, go for great fabrics since they will go the distance. An elegant cashmere sweater or shawl will last for decades if you treat it with care, and a classic tweed jacket can get you through a lifetime of winters. One simple silk shirt can be all business with a suit or dressed up for cocktails, while a gabardine Burberry raincoat will keep you dry and looking smart. Fashions come and go, but fine fabrics never go out of style.

One caveat: The swing and flow of delicate fabrics are visually appealing, but a woman who knows The Ropes will check for transparency and keep a supply of slips and camisoles in case there's something sheer that you just must have. Best leave a little to the imagination.

Your Personal Best

Once you honestly determine what look is good for you, start your quest to find perfect examples of that style. Don't get sidetracked by impulse buying. I don't care how great the bargain is, I don't want you to buy something that isn't perfect for you ever again!

Then, get rid of all the stuff that's *always* been too small, too short, too tight, or just too ugly. If it's too young or too trendy, give it to your niece. Give the rest to charity because someone out there needs clothing. However, if it was really expensive, sell it on eBay!

Oh, and by the way, we all know that our bodies

change as we get older, but that doesn't mean that you have to resign yourself to wearing tents or keeping your shirt permanently untucked. Check out the previous chapter, "Size Doesn't Matter," and get your fashionista groove on.

By the time you hit sixty, you should be able to reach into your closet and grab anything, knowing that it's going to look absolutely fabulous on you.

Nips and Tucks and Shots, Oh My!

What you need to know about cosmetic surgery

> *I want to grow old without facelifts.*
> *I want to have the courage to be loyal*
> *to the face I have made.*
> —MARILYN MONROE

To lift or not to lift? That is the question. It's not always affordable or practical. The very idea of a sharp instrument near the face is an anathema to some women. But there are many different forms of "nonsurgical plastic surgery," as well as some relatively safe surgeries that you might consider.

Nearly 150,000 facelifts were performed in the United States in 2004.

In the nonsurgical department, one of the latest is thermage, a technique that uses radio waves to tighten the skin. Thermage costs around $2,500 and lasts from six months to two years. Traditional facelift surgery costs between $7,000 and $15,000 and lasts five to ten years. With thermage, the radio waves are used to heat the middle and deep tissue layers of the skin and thus stimulate the growth of collagen. The surface of the skin is constantly cooled during the procedure. Generally, there is a noticeable difference immediately and, as the collagen level increases, the effect is more dramatic up to six months after the procedure. The bad news is that it doesn't work for everyone and there is no way to tell if it will work for you. On the upside, with thermage you can go back to your normal routine the same day, whereas with a surgical facelift the recuperation time is at least two weeks.

Collagen injections have become rather commonplace over the past twenty years and they work wonders on those vertical lines that connect your nose to your mouth. The lasting effect varies, but you can count on at least a couple of months. The price varies by the amount of collagen used in the treatment.

Some women prefer fat injections. One of Hugh

Hefner's girlfriends had fat removed from her buttocks and injected around her cheekbones. Then all the other girls who were lower on the food chain said after giving her a respectful peck on the cheek that they were tired of kissing her ass.

The latest, most expensive, and most durable injection is Restylane. It acts rather like collagen but it's not an animal-based material so you needn't wait for allergy testing, even if it's your first time. It's primarily used to pump up lips and those basset hound grooves down the side of your mouth (nasolabial folds, to be precise). Restylane starts at about $500 per syringe, and that doesn't go very far. But it lasts twice as long as collagen so you only need to get it done a couple of times a year.

Can't You Tell I'm Frowning?

And of course, there's Botox and all its close relations. It's not a procedure for injection weenies, as it's fairly painful, but it's very effective. Injected into the forehead, it erases the frown lines between your eyes, the vertical lines on your forehead, and even gives a bit of an eyelift. For some women the effects are immediate, but depending upon the doctor and the patient, it can take up to two weeks to see the full results. That'll cost you about $400, and you can add another couple of hundred to have your crow's feet relaxed.

You can even accomplish some minimal neck tightening with Botox, but you can't use it around your mouth or you'll end up talking like Sylvester Stallone. But, a skillful physician can use a minimal amount in the vertical lines in the upper lip to help train your lips not to purse.

As tempting as it is to have your injections at a party or the gym, use a real dermatologist or plastic surgeon. Botox relaxes (okay, paralyzes) muscles, and there's always a slight risk that you'll end up with a droopy eye if the injections aren't precisely placed, so make sure the person wielding the needle really knows what he's doing. The best way to find a doctor who can do that is to get a recommendation from someone who has had some Botox work done. Just look for someone your age with a forehead so smooth that it looks as if a worry has never passed through her brain. It's up to you how you get them to confess that they've had anything done at all.

The best thing about Botox is that it isn't permanent. If you don't like the effect you don't have to live with it forever. There are newer injections available that promise permanent results, but you must remember that if you have something inserted in the lines in your face the aging process still continues and you may have quite a different result in ten years. Remember the repercussions of the silicone injections that were so popular in the sixties? One famous model that had silicone injected directly into her face has a perfectly unlined visage at the age of sixty-five, but the poor thing can't stop blinking—she's a human strobe light.

Celebrities and beauty mavens have long used electrical stimulation, very similar to the technique used for electronic muscle stimulation and pain relief. With a good technician, results are immediate. You can actually walk out the door looking significantly lifted. The downside is that it's expensive—a couple of hundred bucks each time—and you pretty much have to do it every week. But if money and time are not issues with you, this could be the way to go.

It's in Your Hands

As we all know, ladies, it's not just the face that shows our age. My disc jockey friend told me about being approached by a fan who appeared to be about her age.

"Whoa, man," the guy said. "When I heard you on the radio talking about being friends with Janis Joplin and such, I thought you must be ancient! Then I saw you here and I said to myself no way it could be true, 'cuz you look so young! Then I saw your hands."

"I was mortified," she said. "It turned out the guy was only forty although he had skin like ten yards of corduroy. As for me, I wore gloves for the next three weeks. It was a real glamour buzz kill." Yes, my lovelies, the hands are traitorous. The elbows are also a dead giveaway, but only drastic (and might we add weird) surgery can deal with those wrinkly rascals. However, we can give our mitts a helping hand. While we can't do much about the plumped up veins that come with age, we most certainly can address those nasty little brown bits that were once called "liver spots" or "age spots." Now they are referred to as pigmented lesions and are easily disappeared. Back in the day, your dermatologist would freeze them off with liquid nitrogen, leaving you with a scatter shot of tiny scabs that made it look as if you had been on a naked bacon-frying spree.

Modern photo facial treatments can remove those spots from entire areas—face, chest, forearms, hands, wherever—and usually in a single session. There's minimal pain, just a tingly sensation or a little zap and you're left with a bit of residual redness in most cases. It's all done with pulsed light that breaks up the pigment in the lesions, and it's even faster than lasers. Much as with thermage, the full results of the photo facial treatments don't show up immediately. First the lesions darken slightly and then they begin to fade away in a couple of weeks. You have to keep the whole area constantly moisturized, and the darkest of the dark spots will usually develop a toasty little crust that wipes away in the shower after about ten days.

The photo facial is also great for getting rid of vascular lesions. Those would be the creepy little spider veins that show up on your face, particularly around the nose, giving you the look of a full-color road map.

One of the more embarrassing and common skin problems that worsens with age is rosacea, that bright red facial inflammation that the television commercials are always blathering about. Talk about a hot flash! One bite of spicy food or even a glass of wine can make your whole face light up like Rudolph's nose. It turns out that rosacea is another condition that can be easily treated with photo facial techniques.

Another popular and quick nonsurgical procedure

is LED photomodulation. It's similar to pulsed light but much milder. Accordingly, the results are not as dramatic, but it's perfect for reducing fine wrinkles around the eyes and mouth. This one you can do during lunch, reapply your makeup, and still have time to stop for a latte on the way back to work.

Legend has it that Marlene Dietrich used needles and thread to give herself a temporary facelift.

New technologies and techniques are being developed every day, such as the thread lift. This nonsurgical, no-scar facelift uses a small needle to insert tiny surgical sutures or threads (called prolene sutures) in the same areas where a surgeon would cut for a facelift. The threads have little barbs that grab onto droopy tissue, which is then lifted and repositioned. The threads stay within the deep fat and subcutaneous tissue forever, as they are nonabsorbable and provide support and prevention against further aging. There are rarely any complications, but make sure you select someone with a great deal of experience with the procedure, because if the threads aren't positioned properly, they can leave some unsightly bumpy lines along the edges of your face.

The Cutting Edge

Now let's discuss The Big Knife. If you decide you're ready for actual plastic surgery, make sure you do your homework. I had my eyes done about fifteen years ago, and I've always been sorry. I didn't know the right questions to ask and, in hindsight, I realize I was embarrassingly uninformed. Worse, I've never been happy with the way the surgery changed the look of my eyes. Even now, so many years later, when I look at myself in the mirror, I don't always recognize the woman staring back at me.

> *Eyelid surgery is the fourth most popular cosmetic surgery—outranked by nose job, breast augmentation, and liposuction.*

I lucked out on my neck, though. I never really had one of those tight, firm necks, and I was in severe danger of looking like a bloodhound in a few years, so I did it around the same time I did my eyes. Luckily, the "cleaning up of the jawline" worked wonders, and I've not had to do anything to my neck since. It is the one surgery that probably makes the most dramatic difference aside from a full facelift. The newest neck procedure is the "quick lift," a surgery performed with a very shallow cut around the front of the ear and just behind the earlobe. It involves pulling the neck muscle upward. You should be cleared to go about your life in twenty-four hours without so much as a Band-Aid.

Be smart. Do your homework and make sure you ask the right questions.

Here are some questions to put on your checklist.

1. ASK: Are you certified by the American (or other country) Board of Plastic Surgeons? A simple yes is not enough. You need to know what board and you need to call to confirm. Trusting is not an option here.

2. ASK: Do you have hospital privileges, and where? You don't want some quack operating only out of the office, although many procedures are easily performed in the office. The hospital will have knowledge of his training and competency. If he doesn't have a hospital reference, run away.

3. ASK: How many times have you performed this procedure? This question is especially important if this is a new technique. ASK to see certificates

of his training. Most people are timid when it comes to asking doctors about their experience. This is the only face and body you have. If the doctor screws it up you'll regret it for the rest of your life while malpractice insurance will cover his or her butt.

4. ASK: What is my recovery time and exactly what are the postoperative procedures? You need to know how much time and care to give yourself, because if you don't, you may lose many of the benefits of the surgery.

5. ASK: What are the risks of the surgery? Well, duh, there are always risks to surgery, but if you have any preexisting medical conditions, you could die from a nose job.

6. ASK: What about scars and where will they be? Believe it or not, the formidable scars from something like a tummy tuck might be more of a turnoff for both you and your lover than that little belly was. If you have an augmentation or a reduction, there will be scars under your breasts; there's no getting around it. Consider how your scars have healed in the past. Do you still have

that one from when your little brother acciden-
tally stuck you with the scissors? Hmmmm. . . .

7. ASK: What if it doesn't go right? What if I don't
   like the results? What if it doesn't come out like
   you said it would? You need to know if you have
   recourse, if the surgeon is willing to perform a
   redo, and at what, if any, charge.

8. ASK: The hardest questions are the ones you
   should ask yourself. Why do I want to do this? Is
   it because I want to be young forever? Because I
   want to relive my past? Or, maybe, just maybe, it's
   that I'd like to look really good in my last three
   decades. . . .

Keep in mind that there's more than one way to accomplish your cosmetic goals. Above all, beware of
bargain hunting. It's your face. You're going to get
what you pay for.

Also, consider having some fun while you're getting lifted. There are even facelift "safaris" in South
Africa. You recuperate on a game preserve with the
sounds of jungle birds to lull you to sleep and wildlife
cavorting outside your window. The surgeries are performed by very reputable doctors, but you want to be

sure to check them out thoroughly before throwing yourself to the lions.

Every woman wants to be the very best version of herself, so go ahead and have your neck done, your ears pulled back, or whatever procedure you're contemplating, but don't make surgery a habit. I have a friend who has had her breasts reduced and inflated so many times she's threatening to have flip-top nipples installed. Just fix it once and then let yourself age gracefully.

It's most important to avoid Scary Clown Syndrome (SCS). You know the look—big puffy lips, skin pulled back so tight you smile when you bend over, eyes tilted up at the corners, and way too much makeup. Don't be the older woman of whom it's said, "One more facelift and she'll have a goatee."

Hello, He Lied

What a man is really saying

Chris Rock says that all a man is ever saying is one thing, "Would you like some d**k?" As he opens your door, pulls out your chair, whatever, under his breath he's really saying, "Would you like a little d**k with that?"

If you assume up-front that some part of everything a man says is a lie, you'll always be right. It's just understanding which part is the lie and which, if any, is the truth. It's rather like determining which male head is doing the thinking, not usually too difficult a task. It's amazing how sincere a man can seem when there's not a germ of veracity coming out of his mouth. Many of them get so good at it that they actually believe themselves. Women may fake orgasms, but only men are truly capable of faking a relationship.

It's not that we don't lie, we just lie more indirectly. To our girlfriends about our brand-new designer dress: "This? I've had it so long I can't even remember where I bought it." Or to the penurious husband: "Every time I wear this dress you ask me if it's new." This last bit is best followed up with a peck on the forehead or an affectionate tousling of his thinning hair. Unlike men, we women actually *know* when we're lying. Some women will lie about their shoe size—smaller of course—although it's a mystery as to why. It's not as if there are legends about the correlation between a woman's foot size and the size of her, well, you know. Men will lie up a size or two, as if their sexual prowess is somehow connected to their feet. A man's feet are really important to women only when they are being used for the purpose of walking down the aisle or two miles to the gas station after we've forgotten to check the gas gauge.

Most of us have, at one time or another, lied about our age, if only to get served in a bar. Men, however, lie pretty much on spec, and for only one basic reason. To get over, to get laid, to score. "How about some d**k with that?"

Men lie about how much money they make, whether or not they are married, how many ex-wives (or current wives) they have, how hard they work, where they went to school, and whether or not they've slept with your best friend. So how do we deal with the lies? Ah, there are so many lies, but also many solutions to the sting of being lied to.

The trouble with some women is that they get all excited about nothing—and then marry him.

— CHER

The most painful lie is the cheating husband who says he's never going to lie to you again. Or the one that tells you he'll always be there for you and then dumps you for his bimbo of an assistant. Personally, my reaction to that sort of thing will always be the most base: a desire for revenge. When my husband's girlfriend wrote a book called *How I Survived My Boyfriend's Divorce,* I was furious. Then one night I heard her on a radio talk show and I called in. I told the screener that I was writing a book called *How I Survived My Husband's Girlfriend's Book.* They put me on the air, much to her chagrin. I enjoyed this harmless and entertaining bit of revenge and dined out on it for months.

For the single woman, there is the lie of absence. If a man disappears from your life for a couple of weeks or on weekends, you can be fairly sure he's seeing some other woman. Or women. Depending on how you feel about him, and whether or not you're practicing safe sex, you may or may not want to put him on the spot about it. If you're not serious about him, you may not want to know. The truth not only hurts, it could destroy a great sexual fling or handy casual affair. Besides, even if he does tell you he's seeing someone else, it's unlikely that you'll ever know the whole truth about that.

That Familiar Ring

There's also the possibility that he's married. I don't do married men myself, although these days I seem to attract them like I'm wearing some weird sort of flypaper. An amazing number of them start right out with, "I'm married," which will be the last truthful statement to come for about thirty minutes, during which he'll go through the litany of whys that are somehow supposed to make it okay for you to sleep with him. Wife is mean, cheats on him, got fat, he still loves her but not in "that way," and the shopworn but still classic bit about how she doesn't understand him. The creepiest one is the man who says his wife is dying of cancer or some other dread disease and he's just soooo lonely. That one made me want to open a vein, and not one of my own.

A husband is what's left of the lover after the nerve has been extracted.

— HELEN ROWLAND

Ever wonder about those guys who manage to maintain multiple wives and families for years until somehow they get tripped up? You know, they forget which set of kids goes with which spouse and start calling one of them "Bunnytoes" instead of "Sugarlips." How do these guys handle the money demands of two families? I suppose all he has to do is earn a bunch of it and hand it over to the wives and leave running the household(s) to them. What is it that drives a man to do such a thing? Oh, yes, I remember now: the little head. "I love you, Bunnylips, er, toes. Would you like a little d**k with that?"

Bad Lies, Good Lies

Can it possibly be that we women are that gullible, or is it just that we *want* to believe our man is faithful? Our self-worth is so tied to men that we allow them to get away with lies we wouldn't accept from a ten-year-old child, which is, of course, what most men are.

You don't actually have to fall for each and every tall tale. And it's kind of fun to just let it go if you are only casually dating. Next time he tries the grown-up version of "a giant orange caterpillar ate it," try giving him an amused smirk and a look that says, "I know you're lying, but I don't give a rat's ass." It can work wonders. It may not actually make him tell the truth, but it'll make him squirm, which can be a real pleasure to watch. Don't interrogate him or try to catch him out, just let it go. But not without giving him *that look*. And you can be even more amused as he tries a different sort of tale the next time he needs an excuse.

Not all lies are bad. Some lies are just plain flattering. For instance, if a man tells you you're beautiful on a day when you have a humongous headlight pimple on the end of your nose or when you feel every year of your age, go with it. If you're fifty-five and someone tells you that you don't look a day over forty, just believe it. And you can feel free to be thrilled when a younger man tacks a few years on his age when trying to put the make on you. At least then you know that you don't have to lie about *your* age.

A man can sleep around, no questions asked, but
if a woman makes nineteen or twenty mistakes,
she's a tramp.

— JOAN RIVERS

The best defense against the natural male proclivity
for prevarication is to be prepared. Then, if he actually
tells you the truth, you can be pleasantly surprised.

Men are, after all, quite useful. They can reach for
stuff on the top shelf, explain the finer points of football, pump gas when you're wearing a formal gown,
and squash those creepy bugs that scare the bejeepers
out of you. They are especially adorable when they give
you presents, and they are fun to kiss.

Besides, a side order of d**k isn't all that bad
sometimes.

The Pause That Depresses

Or, Menopause—The Final Insult

> *I'm out of estrogen and I have a gun.*
>
> —T-SHIRT SLOGAN

*I*t happens to all of us, it creeps up on us—and not on little cat feet. More like size fourteen jackboots. It comes up behind us when we least expect it and stomps us into the ground. It's menopause, and it makes puberty look like a day at Disneyland without the funny hats. For every day you ranted about the unpleasantries of your menstrual cycle, you will spend ten menopausal ones wishing you could have those bloody days, as it were, back again.

The average age for the onset of menopause is fifty, but it happens as early as thirty-five and as late as sixty.

Over 5,400 of us get on this bus every day in the United States, and not one damned one of us is sure where we're going. Now, if we live past fifty-four, we're probably going to make it all the way to eighty-four. That means that up to half of our lives will be lived after menopause, so we'd better get a handle on how to deal with it.

Smoke Signals

Oh, the list of ailments that accompany the so-called change of life. Your formerly succulent ya ya starts to dry up and shrivel like a slice of mango left out in the sun, your skin feels like it's stretched over a drum, and you can almost feel your boobs sagging another millimeter each day. One day you look in the mirror and realize if you start getting any more superfluous facial hair, you're going to be eligible for a lead in *The Werewolf of Nordstrom*. On the upside, winters are much cozier now that you have those convenient hot flashes.

There's a sort of temporary insanity that sets in, as I can clearly see with my hindsight bifocals. It was my fiftieth birthday, and my husband, David, had been planning a lavish bash. He'd kept the details secret and asked only that I drop a photo by the printer to be included in the invitation he'd designed.

I didn't have a photo that I really felt expressed the true me, so I called a well-known celebrity photographer (who has, thankfully, gone on to that great photo shoot in the sky) and arranged for a quick session. I chose to wear a leather motorcycle jacket, a thong, and a pair of high-heeled boots with some rather kinky-looking buckles. The photographer made me an instant print and I dropped it off at the printer.

My husband, always trusting my good taste (which apparently had been kidnapped by the Menopause Bandits), had the invitations sent out without even previewing the photo. I thought no more about it, at least until the R.S.V.P.'s and accompanying commentary started choking up the answering machine. Looking back, I would say that was the beginning of the end of my marriage.

And then there are the mood swings. Ah, I can almost hear you shrieking, "WHAT MOOD SWINGS?" My friend, the food critic, once hit a man over the head with a plate of shrimp because he suggested the chef might have used a bit too much garlic. "And that, your honor, was when I decided to try hormone therapy," she said. "My shrimp pills," she calls them. They've helped, she admits, but she's still not welcome in that restaurant.

What dreadful hot weather we have! It keeps
me in a continual state of inelegance.

— JANE AUSTEN

There are subtle clues that indicate you're experiencing the "pause," but they're often hard to pick up on
when you're contemplating murdering your lover and
wondering if menopause is a plausible defense. It's the
fleeting thoughts that should tip you off. For instance, if
you find yourself imagining what it would be like to
just pack up one suitcase, get a phony ID, and board a
tramp steamer bound for the Bahamas, you might be
experiencing menopause. If you're stuck in traffic and
find yourself fantasizing about running over other
drivers with an armored vehicle, you just could be in
the Menopause Zone. And any thoughts of sending out
a birthday invitation with a picture of you in a thong
and leather boots . . .

Kicking Mother Nature's Butt

Fortunately, there are lots of different ways to fight
back against this hideous prank of Mother Nature.

There's much ado about hormone replacement therapy. Aside from what modern science has to offer, there are menopause remedies ranging from diet to exercise, from medicine to myth. Experiment with anything that won't actually harm you and you will probably find what works for you. Read everything you can and make your own decision. At the very least you'll stay too busy doing research to contemplate killing your lover.

Hormone replacement isn't for every woman. Studies are constantly changing the news about HRT, and it's pretty hard to keep up. It seems as if every few months a new study comes out that contradicts the last one. It's scary and confusing.

Every woman's hormonal needs are different, so you'll have to find a program that works for you. I can only tell you what has worked for me and for my friends. If you can't afford a specialist or your health care program doesn't pay for hormone therapy (although it probably pays for Viagra), check out your local free women's clinic. Although these clinics are primarily designed to provide birth control for those who can't afford it, you can get a professional opinion, a reference, and often a prescription for a modest donation. Many of the doctors are women (because we volunteer) and they are more likely to be receptive to your situation.

Some say that having a male gynecologist is like having a mechanic who has never owned a car.

After hearing so many frightening stories about the risk of breast cancer and heart disease in connection with standard synthetic hormone therapy, I questioned my wonderful gynecologist about a more natural approach. He created a cocktail for me made up of bioidentical hormones, hormones that are exactly like the ones the human body normally produces, and I thank him silently every morning. I feel supple and energetic, and I really do think that my tailor-made hormone therapy is a big part of it. My positive attitude allows me to wake up in the morning and plunge myself into my workout routine with gusto and, occasionally, even joy. In turn, the exercise cranks my energy level up a couple of notches, creating (according to some of my nearest and dearest) a downright annoyingly sunny outlook on the rest of my day.

I can't recommend a specific therapy for you, because every woman's "pause" is as unique and individual as a snowflake (which would melt if it got near me at fifty). I have one friend that I envied for twenty years because she was one of those rare females—a medical anomaly—who did not have regular menstrual periods. The most she ever experienced was a few spots every other month, light enough to be handled with a couple of cotton pads in her panties. She had never experienced cramps or PMS, so when she was bitchy I knew she was just a bitch with no excuse. Oddly, she was so incredibly fertile that she could get pregnant just by looking at a man, and all her babies were born by Caesarean section since she never had labor pains! I thought she was the luckiest woman in the world until she called me shortly after her fiftieth birthday. She had just started a relationship with a marvelous man and after two nights of passion, she'd suddenly begun bleeding bright red. Fearing the worst, she rushed to her longtime gyno. "Welcome to our world," her gyno smirked. "This is your version of menopause."

I have to admit that I was relishing the payback aspect, especially when she started having crippling cramps every month. Then I realized how fortunate I was to have gone through that hideous monthly torture when I was young. I was able to comfort my friend in her time of need, to tell her about the exercises, the best nonprescription medication, the tampons, the whole nine yards. I got to show a fifty-year-old friend the tips about menstruation. You might say I showed her The Ropes.

Hormonework

The best approach to hormone therapy is to start reading everything you can find about the subject and then seek out a doctor that specializes in the field of hormone replacement. There are quite a few prescription and nonprescription creams and patches that deliver the hormones while bypassing the liver, which many doctors believe is a safer method. Some of the nonprescription compounds are available online, but you really have to be sure you understand how the various hormones interact with one another—for instance, you *must* take progesterone if you are taking estrogen, and it's a good idea to stay away from creams that contain both, as you may end up getting too much in either direction.

If you are already taking synthetic hormones and you want to switch to bioidentical therapy, it's a good idea to taper off the synthetics rather than quit cold turkey. The shock of being deprived of its usual high dose of medication will most likely send your body back into the unpleasant world of hot flashes and mood swings, and nobody who has experienced that particular form of hell is eager to revisit it.

The menopausal symptoms and their severity vary wildly from woman to woman. Some have found great relief as close as their local health food store. Big favorites are ginseng and kava for moodiness, black cohosh for hot flashes, valerian for insomnia, and good old green tea for energy. It sure couldn't hurt to take calcium and magnesium to keep your old bones healthy and strong. In any case, at this time in your life you should be conscious of proper nutrition and, if you haven't already done so, you should develop a regular vitamin and supplement regimen. It's sort of like maintaining a vintage Corvette or Ferrari. There's no point in spending time and money to keep the exterior in prime condition if you let the interior deteriorate and never change your oil. After all, you don't want to just cruise around and show off your body (although that's now even more fun than when you were fresh off the lot). No, you want to *drive* this baby in comfort and style and you want to leave those other newer models standing still at the starting line. Vroom.

Ladies Who Lunch

*Lasting relationships between
women friends*

It's the friends you can call up at 4:00 A.M. that matter.
—MARLENE DIETRICH

re you one of the lucky ones who has had the same best girlfriend since high school or college, or maybe even elementary school? Women can remain friends throughout the changing circumstances in their lives—marriage, divorce, career changes, even moving far away from one another.

This is not to say that, despite opinions to the contrary, we can't be great friends with men as well, but there is something truly special about getting together with a gal pal and doing what we do best: listen to each other. Sure, we actually do talk a lot more than men, but we are also the better listeners. Men, at least when dealing with women, seem to think that the opposite of talking is waiting to talk again. For women, talking is the essence of relationships. Unlike men, we don't get together to talk about sports or vent about work. We tend to dive into more personal topics like relationships and family, and our conversations are not so much about stating our opinions but rather processing information as we talk. We work things out as we go along, making connections as we take in the thoughts of others, allowing ourselves to reconsider the problem or situation. Also, we have this odd ability to talk and listen at the same time. Men are totally befuddled by this exclusively feminine skill of *receptive conversation*. They just think we're both talking at the same time and not hearing what the other is saying. In fact, we're taking multitasking to a new level.

Women can talk and listen simultaneously. Men find this baffling.

Unless you have a steady boyfriend, chances are you spend a considerable amount of time alone, looking for ways to enjoy your life. If you don't already have a network of fabulous girlfriends, get busy putting one together. If you have only one girlfriend and she's busy, what will you do with that extra ticket to the symphony that you got from your boss? How can you get a four-some for a great game of bridge if you only have one friend? Let's face it, women have a lot to offer on the friendship level. Not only do they share that specialized knowledge about things that are exclusively female, but they also know about cars, computers, the stock market, movies, gardening, and even sports. I ask you, where are you going to find a man who can fix your flat as fast as Morgan Fairchild, who can change a tire in record speed? And even if he could, would he be able to gossip about the latest celebrity wedding at the same time, all while wearing high heels?

Good communication is just as stimulating as black coffee, and just as hard to sleep after.

— ANNE MORROW LINDBERGH

Lunch is an important girlfriend activity, and it's even better when combined with a little shopping. Even the busiest of us will find time to share a salad and per-haps a glass of expensive sparkling water with a female friend, especially if one of us has discovered an adorable new restaurant. Young girls will squabble about the check and who had what, but grown-up women who know

The Ropes will split it down the middle or take turns picking up the tab if they get together regularly. Women with long-term friendships go through different economic phases, and usually the one who has the most money at the time will offer to make it her treat, knowing that her generosity will be repaid.

Friendships between young girls usually have elements of competition and jealousy that often result in brief estrangements and even the occasional catfight that men fantasize about. But if the relationship survives and matures along with the women, these destructive elements fade away and the memories of those silly squabbles serve to bring us closer together.

Friends in Need, Indeed

As I approached fifty I began to value my female friendships more than ever. Then when my marriage began to disintegrate, I turned to these women not just for consolation but also for their wisdom. Through them, I was able to tap into a sort of specialized knowledge that helped me to deal with events that I felt had truly demolished my life. Even women I hadn't seen for a long time stepped up to the plate. They took pains to elevate me from a hideous depression by insisting that I accompany them to parties, art-gallery openings and, of course, lunch. When I finally emerged from my funk, I expressed my gratitude to each and every one of them, for I know I wouldn't have survived without them.

A friend is one who knows all about you and likes you anyway.

— CHRISTI MARY WARNER

There is almost nothing a woman won't share with her best friend, except for her man and possibly her shoes, if only just the expensive ones. We wouldn't think twice about lending a car or a food processor, and we've even been known to cough up our most important piece of jewelry for a friend's special event. We'll share our clothing, although a good friend knows what *not* to try to borrow, like something you just bought and have worn only once. She'll wait until you've stopped wearing it every chance you get, then she knows pretty soon you'll be asking if she wants to borrow it.

Sigmund Freud asked, "What do women want?" Silly man, the answer is shoes!

What is it with women and shoes? I know, if God didn't want us to wear high heels she wouldn't have made our legs look so good in them.

But there seems to be something more primal about the actual hunt for footwear, as if we are lionesses on the prowl. Only in this case, we are not hunting for the pride, but for instant gratification. Two women in search of shoes are bonded perhaps as closely as they ever will be, unless they are both vying for the same perfect pair of pumps, in which case friendship goes right out the window in favor of every woman for herself.

I dress for women. I undress for men.

— ANGIE DICKINSON

You Don't Always Need a Man

As we get older, our female friendships deepen, until finally we even occasionally pass up the opportunity for male companionship in favor of time with someone of the same sex. While there's no evidence that even the older single woman ever stops looking for a man to share her life with, as we get older we seem to be more comfortable taking a little time off from the hunt and relaxing with our pals.

Collaborating on creating a fabulous light lunch and sipping tea out on the deck on a Sunday afternoon is a great alternative to sitting around watching the guys watch football. Besides, on any day that men are entranced by sports, it's unlikely there's any romance in the cards for you.

Laugh and the world laughs with you. Cry and you cry with your girlfriends.

—LAURIE KUSLANSKY

There are times when women want to see only women. When you're in the hospital, for instance, hair askew, wearing that dreadfully unflattering gown that exposes your dimpled ass, who do you want by your side—the guy you're dating who thinks of you as a sex goddess or your best girlfriend who not only won't care how you look but knows the right questions to ask your doctor?

A Tip of The Hat

If you find yourself shy of girlfriends who like to go out and have a good time, perhaps you might like to join an existing network. The Red Hat Society is a group of over-fifty women across the United States who meet at least once a month to share everything from poetry to pancakes, bowling to banquets. Everyone wears an outrageous red hat and a purple dress as a means of identification, and these women turn heads wherever they go.

The original red hat was purchased in Tucson, Arizona, in 1997 in a thrift store, and the organization was created by Sue Ellen Cooper. Since the Red Hat Society's inception in 1998, it's grown to 36,000 chapters and 850,000 members, so there's sure to be a group near you. The society has spawned a best-selling book, has twenty-six licensing deals, and sells hundreds of products through department stores and specialty shops.

The Red Hat Society began as a result of a few women deciding to greet middle age with verve, humor, and élan. We believe silliness is the comedy relief of life, and since we are all in it together, we might as well join red-gloved hands and go for the gusto together. Underneath the frivolity, we share a bond of affection, forged by common life experiences and a genuine enthusiasm for wherever life takes us next.

—SUE ELLEN COOPER, QUEEN MOTHER

While you are allowed to join the Red Hat Society before you're fifty, you must hit that five-decade mark before you earn the honor of sporting the red chapeau. Until then, young ladies, you must be content with a pink lid. But have no fear; you'll be welcomed into the group with open arms. After all, girls—no matter the age—just wanna have fun!

And remember, men don't live as long as women, so cultivate those female friends. They may be the only ones left in the end.

Prep Time and Debriefing

The care and feeding of forty-plus skin

> *The less I behave like Whistler's Mother the night before, the more I resemble her the next day.*
>
> —TALLULAH BANKHEAD

*J*ust as the list of redeeming qualities we hope for in a man gets shorter over time, the list of beauty preparations gets longer. The older we get the longer it takes to get ready to go to bed and to get out of the house in the morning. After the fifty mark, it's more about preservation; once I hit sixty, I actually considered washing my face with formaldehyde instead of water.

Beauty Debriefing at Night

The night is a time-vampire as far as taking care of your skin goes. Everything that has wrought itself upon your face and body must be undone, whether it was inflicted by your own hand (makeup, alcohol, laziness) or by nature (air pollution, sun, allergies). No matter who or what is to blame, you are the only person who can help you. You can start to do that by placing yourself smack in front of the magnifying mirror in your bathroom. Here is where you examine yourself more closely than a customs inspector, and you don't just look at your bags.

First, you must find the time to make sure to rid your face of every wonderful beauty-enhancing product you've slathered on it. It doesn't matter how expensive the eye shadow or foundation, once nighttime sets in, these once-beautifying concoctions become poison to your skin. Same goes for the body—leg or scar makeup, for instance. Just get it all off so that your skin has a chance to breathe overnight.

Gone are the days when you wear a bit of makeup in bed so that your man never gets to see the barefaced you. That kind of superficial and temporal vanity has a price. Pimples and wrinkles are just the tip of the iceberg. You need to keep your skin clean and moisturized as much of the time as you can manage for it to hold up longer. In this respect, women are like automobiles, and let's face it, we're older models—if not quite vintage—and it's not as if we can cover up everything with a seat cover after thrashing the original upholstery.

So, let's start at the top. If your hair is getting thinner than the line between love and lust, consider that old tried-and-true method of one hundred strokes of the hairbrush to stimulate the scalp. If you're sleeping alone, give your hair a conditioning treatment while you sleep. You needn't spend a lot of money on it, either. A tablespoon of olive oil rubbed into your locks may cause you to slip off the bed in the middle of the night, but when you wash your hair in the morning it'll have an extra sheen.

Now for the face. Pull your hair back from your face with a headband or a clip so that you can have full access to the canvas (heaven forbid that be the texture of your skin). No matter if your skin craves a moisturizing cleanser or plain soap and water, you need to make sure that you clean every millimeter of it. And then get it moist, really moist. Even the oiliest of complexions needs moisture. As they say, many things are better when wet.

There's a lot of rubbing of emollients on the body

and the face. You cannot err on the side of too much anointing of the eyes. These are the windows to your soul and they'd better not be cracked and warped like the weathered frames of a New England fisherman's shack. At night you'll want a more intense cream, but in the morning go for something firming.

Pick Your Products

A clever way to try new products before spending a lot of money is to take advantage of the samples available at all department store cosmetics counters. Just ask the counterperson what they have in the way of samples. You can also check out the free gift with purchase that so many companies offer. It's amazing how many tiny tubes of fluids and creams you can amass just while buying mascara.

There is no cosmetic for beauty like happiness.

— MARGUERITE GARDINER,
Countess of Blessington

Experiment with different products until you find what works best for you, but you needn't be a slave to brand names. You can search around the Internet for knockoff brands, many of which are comparable to their more expensive cousins. Diligently do your homework and you can save some bucks while saving your looks. You'll be stunned at how much you can save without sacrificing quality. L'Oréal, for instance, is virtually the same as Lancôme, but at a fraction of the price.

Morning Prep Time

The great reward of performing all these ablutions at night is that you will wake up with a fresh face in the morning. And that brings us to the prep-time section of this chapter. Of course you will have thoroughly cleansed your face upon arising, leaving it slightly moist. Immediately apply your daily moisturizer. The moisturizer helps to keep the water in, hydrating your skin. You know, the last part of a woman's body to get wrinkled is her butt, and the more baths she takes, the less wrinkled her booty is. There are some movie stars who plunge their faces into a basin of cold water while wearing a snorkle. Oh, go soak your face!

You need to have a schedule for your morning prep. Know how long it takes you to get ready and backtime your routine so you'll be out of the house on time. You can be efficient without sacrificing grooming.

Keeping the pores clean is essential, and after you cleanse your face, especially with warm water, your pores are wide open. Pat your skin dry and then run an ice cube over your whole face. Wait for it to dry thoroughly before applying your foundation. Many professional makeup artists and actors use this very trick to protect the skin from heavy theatrical makeup. Also, a fine mist of cold water *after* putting on foundation will set the makeup and help it look fresh longer. Again, wait for any moisture to completely dry before applying a light dusting of powder.

Let's Make Up

Oddly, as we get older, the "less is more" theory comes into play. Less makeup around the eyes will leave you with fewer wrinkles because makeup, particularly undereye concealer, gravitates toward those little lines and fills them up like an overzealous bartender, leaving you with a crinkly expression. And don't go for the light white color—it makes you look like you've been skiing with sunglasses on. Your concealer should be only one shade lighter than your foundation. Also, as we get older, matte makeup of any kind tends to exaggerate wrinkles, so use it sparingly. The real trick is to choose a color that's light enough to cover the dark circles but not so white that you look like you're wearing a costume ball mask. And don't use a greasy pencil to line your eyes because it'll bleed down into the concealer and really make a mess. You can use a bit of translucent powder to set the concealer, but apply it sparingly with a big fat brush instead of a puff. Tap a little powder into the palm of your hand and touch the brush to it, blowing off the excess before you apply.

I've always been a sucker for pricey foundations, but I have found that there are some great inexpensive ones to be had. It's all about figuring out the right shade for your complexion. I always avoid anything with a red or pink tone. These don't blend into the skin color of the neck, and you end up looking apoplectic. I go with a neutral or beige shade so that I can add my own color. If you can find a foundation that goes with your skin tone and also contains a sunscreen or sunblock, so much the better.

There's another area of the body to deal with as far as makeup is concerned. As if Mother Nature hasn't dished out enough esthetic challenges for the mature woman, many of us are coping with those knotty varicose veins. The only way to really get rid of them is through surgery, so if yours are painful or particularly unsightly, you might want to look into that option.

So-called spider veins can be corrected by having your dermatologist inject them with saline solution to seal off the capillaries. Be warned, it's not a painless procedure and it may take several tries before you see any real results.

You might want to do what I do sometimes in the summer when I want to go bare-legged and wear a skirt. There's a wonderful line of body makeup called "Makeup Forever." The colors are quite natural, it goes on easily, and doesn't run off on your clothes (or his). Tanning, of course, is another way to go (see "The Skinny on Skin") but it's really not as effective as makeup.

Tone It Down a Notch

If you ever wore blue eyeshadow, it's better now to think of it as something you used to do but are far too grown up to do now. You need to use a light application of muted neutral colors and put that eyeliner pencil down. The Cleopatra look needs to be set aside.

Ancient Greek women colored their cheeks with a paste of crushed berries and seeds.

Go easy on the blush, too. Always remember you are just one brush stroke away from looking like Bozo the Clown. Those two pink stripes on either side of your face do *not* create the impression of high cheekbones. Rather, it looks like you're wearing war paint. Blend, blend, blend!

Mascara is the trickiest item of all. In the daytime, a light application will be fine. When you start a new tube of mascara, first take the tip and touch it to a piece of tissue to remove the excess gloppiness. And never, ever, pump the wand into the tube. It adds air and dries out the mascara before its time. Take your time with the application so you can coat your lashes separately and you don't end up with Tammy Faye eyes.

The lips are last and, again, let's keep it simple. I find the current trend of pumping up the lips like bicycle tires a desperate and laughable attempt to hang on to a youthful appearance. Unless you actually looked like a duck when you were young, why go there? Let's just try to make do with our real lips.

Lip liner is good for making a perfect mouth, but the trick is to make it look like you didn't line your lips.

Your lip liner should be very close to the color of your lipstick so that you don't look like a page from a coloring book. I know some women who have had their lip liner tattooed on, but I would worry that I would want to change colors later on down the line. I reserve the right to change my mind—and my lip color.

If you're worried that you're not going to be able to do your makeup properly, or that you're just even a little rusty on the current styles and colors, it would behoove you to seek help. It's readily available at your local department store or cosmetics purveyor. Many makeup lines offer periodic free makeovers and consultations, so call and ask around. But don't just have them do your makeup for you—ask a lot of questions and pick up a new skill set.

After the experts have given you a new look, be sure to go out on the town and try it out. Then go home and practice, which will help make you perfect.

Approach your beauty regime like you'd like your man to approach lovemaking: slow, gentle, and thorough. Done right, it can even be fun.

Get Outta Town!

Travel for the single woman

It's a small world until they lose your luggage.
—ANONYMOUS

*I*f your last trip was a fall in the supermarket after some rotten kid knocked over the olive oil display, this chapter is aimed directly at you. Travel not only broadens your horizons figuratively and literally, but it also gives you a chance to meet people, male people even—ones who might appeal to you in a way that your local suitors do not. Plus, the temporal nature of being on the move also means that it's fairly easy to ditch the undesirables, like that loser in the seat next to you who alternated between picking his nose and asking for your phone number throughout the entire flight across the country. If you've packed smart and have only minimal carry-on baggage (we'll discuss packing methodology later in this chapter), you can bolt off the airplane and disappear while he's still cleaning up the detritus that he's strewn about his seat area.

I haven't been everywhere, but it's on my list.

— SUSAN SONTAG

A lot of women don't travel as much as they might because they feel they don't have a suitable companion for the journey. We've all known those brave young women who took off on a solo trek to Europe fresh out of college, staying in hostels and surviving on bread and cheese, but that image doesn't sound quite so glamorous as we get a bit older. A fabulous hotel and a chopped salad with a perfect glass of pinot grigio sounds much more appealing to a woman who knows The Ropes.

Travels with Yourself

We've long since left behind the days of horse and buggy when a woman, no matter her age, might fear for her safety and security when traveling alone. Now we have pepper spray and karate, currency converters and electronic language translators, and nobody better mess with us.

Thirty years ago, women took vacations with husbands and family, but these days more of us are choosing to spend that time with other women. In the new millennium we'll take at least one trip a year with a husband or boyfriend, but 65 percent of women travelers confess to having left the guys at home either to travel with a female friend or to join an all-female tour. Of the women surveyed in a group called Women Traveling Together, 80 percent said they thought that men and women had different ideas, interests, and expectations about vacations. The rest of them said they just felt that men—at least *their* men—weren't all that interested in travel and would just as soon stay home and zone out.

Increasing numbers of both married and single women, especially those who have already blown out forty or more candles on the birthday cake, are choosing to strike out to parts unknown. They're learning to sail in the Bahamas, taking barges down the Nile River, going on archeological digs, and exploring the rainforest. It would seem that more women are seeking new travel experiences and, if they can't get a man to go with them, they'll either go alone or with other like-minded women.

Travel groups catering exclusively to women include Shop Around (yes, shopping trips to Milan and Paris!) and Gutsy Women Travel, a group that offers ecological tours to a rainforest resort specializing in aromatherapy and massage. Don't be too quick to discard the idea of going with a group of older women. They're not necessarily a bunch of grannies in comfy shoes anymore. These older babes can scale a pyramid in Mexico with the best of them, and groups such as the female-only Senior Women's Travel touts itself as being for ladies with large cultural appetites. Their leisurely tours focus on museums, literature, fine dining, and "even finer shopping."

*The number of trips designed especially for women
has more than quadrupled in the last five years.*

There's a difference between traveling and taking a vacation. If you're the kind of babe who just wants to spend two weeks on the beach in Hawaii (wearing a thirty sun-block!), then all you need are a few trashy novels and a couple of bikinis with elegant cover-ups appropriate for sucking down mai tais from hollowed-out pineapples. And if you're going to be in a nice hotel the whole time, you don't really have to worry about bringing, say, a hairdryer and a robe. Just know that going alone to a resort probably isn't going to net you much in the way of real romance, although you might have a fling with the cabana boy.

To Sea or Not to Sea

Ocean cruises have a lot of visual appeal when you see them in a television ad, but by most accounts the experience is not all it's cracked up to be. Despite those images of attractive single people frolicking by the pool and nuzzling over cocktails at the captain's table, a single woman is about as likely to hook up with an unattached man on a party ship as she is to win the lottery, which is about the same odds as being struck by lightning twice. Every summer we seem to hear a flurry of horror stories about backed-up plumbing, mysterious shipboard viruses, and generally ruined vacations. Okay, so you can get your money refunded, but there's no way to get back those weeks that were meant to be magic but turned into tragic.

Above all, try to find out if you are prone to seasickness. The decidedly not fond memories I have from my first cruise are of the ten straight days spent puking my guts out. I did lose a few pounds, but the blood vessels I popped in my face were hideous. After that I never failed to get my Dramamine shot before getting near any sort of seagoing vessel.

You need to find out what seasickness remedy works for you. Some prefer the patch; some like the pills. I know some women who swear by the little acupressure bracelet. Unfortunately, experience is the only true teacher in the icky realm of motion sickness.

But if, despite all the naysaying, a cruise still sounds good to you, there are many from which to choose.

There are cool cruises that are specifically designed for music lovers (the Blues Cruise series), and amateur astronomers can get close to the stars on a special cruise to Alaska. There are cruises specializing in dancing, cooking, literature, film, and even comedy. These events are great learning experiences, and you are much more likely to meet people who share your interests or passions. Vacations needn't involve romance, but it never hurts to gild the lily a bit. It's not that it's impossible to fall in love on a cruise, but don't count on it. And remember, if you travel as a single, the cabin prices are based on two-person occupancy, so the roommate situation is a crapshoot. But if you have a flexible schedule you can wait until the last moment to book and you might just get to be alone in a double cabin. Don't forget that you have bargaining power! Always ask for a deal and you'll more than likely be pleasantly surprised by what discounts can come your way.

Stop worrying about the potholes in the road and enjoy the journey.

— BABS HOFFMAN

Another advantage to these specialized trips is that if you have trouble sticking to a program of taking classes, this is an excellent way to give yourself the discipline to complete the course. After all, short of calling for a helicopter, it's pretty damned hard to get off the boat in the middle of the ocean.

Riding the Rails

Train travel has sort of made a comeback, especially for those who have a fear of flying. Sure, it takes a little—okay, a lot—longer, but it's incredibly relaxing. You can be lulled to sleep by the sound of the churning wheels, and most trains take the scenic route as a matter of course. Unlike most other modes of transportation, getting there is half the fun.

On shorter train trips, it's great fun to just head for the club (bar) car. Here you can get a cocktail and a snack, as well as a livelier party atmosphere. Here's a place to while away the hours with a rousing game of gin or just chat it up with your fellow passengers.

On longer trips, go for a leisurely lunch in the dining car, where you can linger over your coffee as the scenery rolls by. Know, however, that you won't generally be able to get a table all to yourself—space is limited so you'll be expected to share. Train food is a bit pricey and not always really top notch, so if you're traveling on a tight budget, you might want to bring a small cooler and your own little picnic.

Ski train trips are a fabulous winter excursion. You can have an early breakfast on the rails and read the paper or nap until you reach the resort. In many cases you can even buy your lift tickets on the train. Best of all, on the way back you can have a hot toddy and laugh at the poor exhausted skiers fighting the homebound traffic.

It's in the Bag

Whether you're taking a long leisurely seaside vacation, a whirlwind tour to Europe, or just a weekend jaunt to a big city, there are certain essentials that you can learn to tote along. Bring the right stuff and you'll save yourself a world of grief. Moreover, learn to use your suitcase space wisely so you don't need a pack mule to carry your stuff.

With packing, as with love, the little things mean a lot. A small mending kit (save that one from your last hotel stay), a Band-Aid or two, a scrunchy to tie your hair back, sample sizes of toothpaste, sunscreen, and deodorant, and miniature refillable bottles of your favorite shampoo and conditioner are essential. Be sure to label those bottles so you don't end up cleansing your delicate skin with curl relaxer. Store the mini containers in clear sandwich bags and you can always find everything. Also, if you happen to be one of the unlucky souls singled out for a secondary search, the security workers won't make such a mess of your stuff since they can see everything at a glance.

If the trip is more than a few days or to a remote place, I bring a small bottle of nail polish and a tube of superglue for emergency nail repairs. And I'm never without my collapsible sun hat and a thin pair of ballet-style slippers that are equally handy for shuffling around the hotel room or down to breakfast in the morning.

I keep my overnight bag permanently packed with these items and never take them out—that way I don't have to worry about forgetting something. And when I return from a trip, I replenish my supplies so I'll be ready to take off at a moment's notice.

Travel Is My Business

Traveling for business is a completely different animal. You need to be lean, if not mean, and you need to pack even more efficiently. Unless you're going to see the same people every time you travel you can usually get away with a couple of versatile suits. Simply figure out how many meetings you have to attend and who will be there, then choose your number of outfits accordingly.

Here's where polyester comes in handy. Say what you will, polyester doesn't wrinkle and can get you through a long business day a lot better than the most glamorous linen affair. You can find an inexpensive suit at one of those big discount stores and then have it tailored so that it looks like it was made just for you. Pick a roomy jacket with plenty of pockets so that you can tuck your ticket as well as your passport or other ID in a handy pocket for the airline security checks. A looser jacket will also weather long travel times better than something that's snug. At the end of the day, you can add a sparkly turtleneck or a shell with a fabulous necklace and you're ready for the cocktail hour.

Book It, Baby!

When you're traveling for adventure instead of business, you're going to have a whole different set of needs, especially when it comes to planning your itinerary. If you're booking your own trip, you can either use a travel agent or the Internet, depending upon how much time you have. There are some fabulous deals online, but until you become familiar with how to find them, it can take hours to hunt them down. Search engines like Yahoo! have a built-in travel feature that will show you a wide variety of airline ticket prices, or you can search on your own. You'll find you can save hundreds of dollars on flights, hotel rooms, and car rentals. There are tons of unique packages—

like a covered wagon tour of Irish pubs—that you would never even know existed without the Internet, so before you book anything do a lot of comparison shopping. I like to print out the various pages as I find them and then use them for leisurely bedtime reading. For some reason, it all seems more real to me when it's on paper.

It is good to have an end to journey towards, but it is the journey that matters in the end.

—URSULA K. LEGUIN

My favorite part about booking online is the convenience of e-tickets. Now you can not only book and print your ticket online, but most airline sites will allow you to print out your boarding pass twelve hours before your flight. This means if you have only carry-on luggage, you can just go right to the security checkpoint without checking in at the ticket counter. It alleviates that stressed feeling you get when you see the unexpectedly long, serpentine line coiled around in front of the ticket agent and gives you time to stop in the bar for a relaxing but overpriced cocktail and a snack. Remember, they rarely serve food on airlines anymore, unless you count pretzels as a food group. It's a good idea to stash a little bag of trail mix or an energy bar in your carry-on or your purse just in case you find yourself waiting on the runway for a couple of hours. Woman cannot live on airline Bloody Marys alone.

This Trip's for You

The best thing about traveling is that certain annoying parts of everyday life become completely irrelevant for at least short periods of time. If you're on an airplane, for instance, you won't be pestered by telemarketers, door-to-door vacuum cleaner salesmen, or even innocent-looking little Girl Scouts peddling those deadly (to the hips, anyway) Thin Mints. For a few precious hours you can finally be alone with a book or lose yourself in the music with your headsets.

Another bonus is that no one can drop by unannounced and interrupt your valuable nap time. Once you master the art of the airborne nap, you'll look forward to flying as a chance to catch up on your beauty sleep. Be sure to bring some earplugs just in case you're stuck with crying babies or snoring seatmates. I have a phobia about airline blankets—I always imagine I can see the germs through the plastic bag, even if they say they're dry-cleaned after every use. I prefer to bring my cuddly pashmina shawl, which easily doubles as a nap blanket. You may still have trouble getting comfortable, but if you bring one of those little inflatable neck pillows, at least you won't arrive at your destination with a stiff neck.

Just remember that no matter the purpose of your trip, it's up to you to make your travel time pleasant. Be patient, flexible, and cheerful and your journey will be flawless.

The Dating Game

The changing world of dating

I've been on so many blind dates I should get a free dog.

—WENDY LIEBMAN

*D*ating, especially as we get older, is rather like fishing in the dark. Even if you catch something you can't really tell if it's good until you get it home and hold it up to the light. Still, until you've properly prepared it, you can't tell if it will be a tasty dish or just a smelly fish you'll have to toss back in the water.

After my divorce, it was several years before I could even consider going out on a date. It had been twenty-five years since I'd been out with anyone but my husband and I was pretty sure the scene had changed. And I was afraid, very afraid.

I didn't have a clue about where to begin, but you know how girlfriends are when you're suddenly single. I was set up more times than a bowling pin, and my hopes knocked down just as often. My fantasy date was one who could give me an orgasm and start his car in the same moment. I never found him, so I finally decided to go high tech.

Caught in the Net

Where did losers hang out before Internet dating was invented? My friend told me she met thirty-seven potential partners on a dot-com dating service and every single one of them lied about his height. The promise of five feet ten, five feet eleven, or even six feet turned out to be closer to Billy Barty when she opened the front door. What, they thought she wouldn't notice? Well, I guess they figured if she could believe that's what six feet looked like, she'd never question their claims of enormous endowment.

If you are posting your profile online, be honest about yourself. This way you are more likely to meet someone who is compatible.

Anyway, even this parade of geeks did nothing to dissuade her from hounding me to join the ranks of single Women searching the Web for Prince Charming. I held my ground for two years before I finally succumbed.

So, after much fretting and hand-wringing, I created a profile and joined Match.com. I received fifty-eight responses overnight. I read through them (that alone was excruciating) and began the process of elimination. I threw out anyone claiming to be a massage therapist (5), those who couldn't come up with anything better to do than take long walks on the beach (10), and any man who admitted he was seeking a hot-tub encounter (2). Also anyone who wanted to lick me all over or ride me like a pony (just one, thank God). I finished by throwing out anyone who couldn't spell, and I ended up with only four men who were acceptable.

Of the four, only one piqued my interest even slightly. So when my friend wanted a rundown I told her there was really only one prospect that I would consider.

"Tell me about him," she demanded.

I told her he was a professor, age appropriate, lived on the beach in Malibu, and his hobby was photography.

"Oh, you mean Hal," she said.

Hal, my friend had discovered, was a short little

troll who had never even managed to get one of his Internet dates back to his pad, which was probably under a bridge instead of on the beach.

If you decide to go out with someone you've met online, pick a public place to have lunch.

This is not to say that online dating doesn't work. I know some women who swear by it and even a few who have landed husbands that way. Heck, that's how Rush Limbaugh found a bride!

Toad or Prince?

There's no getting around the fact that dating is truly scary, even if you do it all the time. The ratio of toads to princes leans heavily to the warty side, so just try not to date outside your species.

Ah, you say, how to tell the difference? Behold, princesses, a list of the ten most smarmy lines I've ever heard:

1. My name is Steve . . . remember that, because you'll be screaming it later.
2. Hello, I'm Mister Right. Someone said you were looking for me.

3. Hi. The voices in my head told me to come over and talk to you.

4. I lost my phone number. Can I have yours?

5. Nice legs! What time do they open?

6. Are those real? I mean your eyes, of course.

7. That dress is fabulous. It would look even better crumpled in a heap on my bedroom floor.

8. Can I buy you a drink or do you just want the money?

9. If I were you, I'd have sex with me.

10. I know chicks like presents. Wanna open my package?

Really cool guys don't need pickup lines, but just for the sake of this book I asked the most charming, gorgeous, and intelligent men I know to contribute a witticism. Here's what they came up with:

1. I may appear small of stature, but I'm much taller when I stand on my wallet.

2. I'm not ordinarily attracted to women, but you're an exception.

3. I like to shop.

4. You know, you're right!

I ask you, what woman can resist a man who recognizes that she *is* right?

The Cad Factor

You must be observant when wading through the murky waters of the dating pool. The most obvious thing to look for is the wedding ring tan line, although some men are more subtle than others about hiding the wedding ring. A "gentleman" was flirting with me as we were both driving in the same direction on Sunset Boulevard in Hollywood. I had avoided making eye contact with him, but he was so persistent that I finally decided to look at him. Just as I turned my head in his direction he pulled off his wedding ring and tossed it over his shoulder into the backseat. It was as if three letters suddenly lit up on his forehead: CAD.

~~~~~~

A fox is a wolf who sends flowers.

— RUTH WESTON

Meanwhile, resist the feminine temptation to tell him your story chapter and verse (a good idea no matter where you're meeting). Personally, I just don't think I can tell my story to one more person. Even *I'm* bored with it now. Reveal as little as possible. Not only will it make it harder for a possible stalker or cat burglar, it adds a little mystery.

And for heaven's sake, don't go home with him (either his place or yours) the first time you meet. Get yourself to the nearest computer and Google him! See, there's a use for more than one electronic device in your busy life!

Barstool Dating

If you're thinking of looking for love in all the wrong places, namely a bar, you'd do well to remember that movie *Looking for Mr. Goodbar.* Diane Keaton's character comes to a tragic end just because she was a lousy judge of people's intentions, and a little tipsy to boot. These are dangerous times, and it's hard to make a correct snap judgment about a stranger you meet over cocktails, even though they tend not to look so strange after a few martinis.

If you want to catch trout, don't fish in a herring barrel.

— ANN LANDERS, ON SINGLES BARS

You must be moderate in your cocktail consumption. One ounce of booze per hour will keep you legal for the drive home (because you're not letting someone you just met drive you anywhere). Besides, as Raymond Chandler noted, "Class is something that dissolves very quickly in alcohol."

While there's no guarantee that the handsome, charming guy on the barstool next to you isn't a Ted Bundy type, there are certain things you can do to protect yourself. Start by picking a cocktail lounge in a good neighborhood, possibly in a fine hotel. The bad news about the hotel bar is that whoever you meet will likely be an out-of-towner, but at least if it doesn't pan out, you won't have to keep running into him. Try to get to know some other regulars at your tavern of choice so that they might be able to give the inside dish on Mr. Good Stuff. Also, try to see what kind of credit card he's using and make sure you get a complete first and last name. Then you can Google him. See, the computer can be your friend.

A Quick One

One of the more bizarre dating experiences to capture the public imagination is called "speed dating." It's sort a grown-up version of musical chairs, with the woman as the chair. You remain seated with a man across from you, and you have five minutes to pry as much information out of him as you want to know, which sometimes is none at all. When the whistle blows, he moves on and another man takes his place, and so on, and so on. At the end of the session, the participants will have had ten or fifteen five-minute sessions. The women then decide who, if anyone, is worthy of a date.

While five minutes may be sufficient time to determine if a guy's fingernails are clean or if that's actually dandruff on his shoulders, I'm inclined to think the more subtle aspects of human behavior require a bit more time to assess. Even the worst lout can, after all, behave like a perfect gentleman for at least five minutes.

Experts say that the human mind is capable of

instant and instinctively correct judgment. That could be true of those art experts who can tell in a heartbeat if the Getty Museum is about to pay ten million dollars for a fake Italian sculpture, but I'm not sure if it can save you from a fake Italian tycoon.

Finding a Proper Man

There are many more appropriate ways to meet proper men. Oh, sure, everyone says to go to art openings, charity functions, and parties. Some say that weddings are rich territory for male hunting, but you have to consider that it's kind of like being a judge: All the men are wearing suits or tuxedos so it's really hard to tell what they would look like on a regular basis. Unlike the judge, at least you could be fairly sure they wouldn't be changing into an orange jumpsuit after the proceedings.

I require three things in a man. He must be handsome, ruthless, and stupid.

— DOROTHY PARKER

Still, the problem for some women is that actual *meeting* part. The perfect guy might be there right next to the no-host bar or the onion dip, but if you don't send out some kind of signal, you'll never know what could transpire.

Men say that when a woman makes eye contact and then smiles, they melt like a Popsicle on a radiator. Ladies, making eye contact with a man is a very powerful gesture. Meet his eyes. Try not to look away first and certainly not immediately. It says so much about you. It tells a man you are not so shy, not so passive, confident of what you know you can make him feel, that you can make his life more exciting.

Men often find it difficult to look a woman in the eyes. This is because women's eyes are not located in their chests.

— ANONYMOUS

Combine that knowing glance with a smile (another way of telling him and everyone else that you are not oppressed or depressed), and you are instantly riding the wave of a strong sexual aura. Cowabunga!

After that, it's pretty much up to him to ask for your phone number or give you his card. No matter the occasion, I always carry a few discreet, high-quality cards with my phone number (no address) to avoid that tacky business of writing on napkins that are sure to get lost. Of course, that doesn't work when you're trying to give some loser your number with one digit off.

Once the flirting is over and a date is negotiated, it's up to you to make it an evening or day to remember. Naturally, you need to look your best, but make sure it's a look you can replicate on a daily basis. Remember how you looked when he met you. He obviously liked it, so don't go changing too much. If you go for a full professional makeover, he's liable to be startled when you come to the door. "Is your roommate home?" is not the response you're looking for.

Once you're actually on the date, for heaven's sake don't be a Klingon. I don't mean the *Star Trek* creatures with wrinkly brows (we don't want that either, and that's why Botox was invented). I mean the woman who always finds a way to take it all way too seriously, one who needs constant reassurance and attention even on the first date. Most men prefer a woman who isn't needy. Stick to him too closely and you may find yourself being scraped off like gum from the bottom of his shoe.

On the other hand, there's a difference between being confident and being controlling. You can be a strong woman, even an aggressive one, without coming

off like a dominatrix. You don't lose anything by letting
him open a door for you (see page 133) or by letting him
pick the restaurant. Need we mention that passenger-
seat driving is out of the question?

Does this all sound calculated and heartless? Perhaps, but at our age we can't afford to squander even a
few months on a jerk.

I will not go out with a man who wears more
jewelry than me, and I'll never, ever go to bed
with a guy who calls me Babe. Other than that,
however, I'm real flexible.

— LINDA SUNSHINE

It took a few years of dating disasters, but I've managed to hone my instincts and have created an exciting
and stimulating dating life. Here's what it boils down
to: Use your brain—after all, it's considered by many to
be the sexiest organ in the entire body.

Vive la Différence!

Men and women really are from different planets

Men and women, women and men.
It'll never work.

—ERICA JONG

*A*h, men, what would we do without them? Well, for one thing, we'd have to take out the trash and fix our own cars. Oh, wait, we're doing that already! The world of single women is much different these days. We are independent and self-sufficient and darned proud of it. Occasionally, someone will try to make us feel as if we are lacking something if we don't have a permanent man in our lives. When that happens, just remember to keep your sense of humor, an invaluable tool for a woman who knows The Ropes, especially when she's on the dating circuit.

Whether you're looking for a casual affair or a long-term relationship—at any age—the first step to finding the proper man in particular is to understand men in general.

Just the Facts, Ma'am

Men are very different from you and me, and not in just the obvious physical ways. Okay, so we already know that we are from different planets, possibly from entirely separate galaxies. But there are other divergences that keep us from melding together into one species.

Why do you suppose that men are four times more likely to be hit by lightning than women? Well, they do have that built-in lightning rod attached to the torso, but I'm guessing that it's because God is actually a woman. But if that's true, why aren't men the ones having periods and birthing babies? It's all so unfair.

Men are 3 percent more likely to get fat, but we are the ones who worry about it. We do fret about our looks a lot, while men pretty much think they look good all the time. And while the average guy has six to ten toiletry items (including toothbrush and toothpaste) in his bathroom, we women have more like fifty. Admittedly, we don't use all of them on the same day and some have long since passed the expiration date. Many of these products may seem superfluous, but you never know when you're going to need that glitter body spray you bought after a two-martini lunch.

"It was on sale" is always a compelling argument for a woman to buy something she doesn't need. A man, on the other hand, will cough up the cake for even an outrageously overpriced item if he thinks he needs it, especially if it involves electronics. This probably has something to do with the fact that girls pretty much stop playing with dolls when they hit junior high, but boys and their toys can never be separated, no matter how old the boy gets.

I see no need to discuss why it is that men can spend so much time on the toilet, especially with a newspaper. According to a well-known toilet paper company's survey, they prefer to fold their toilet tissue, while chicks crumple. God knows that's the only thing they ever fold aside from the sports page. We women spend at least an hour a day in the bathroom, too, but most of that time is spent in front of a mirror.

Women may seem to obsess about their looks, but we don't just worry about flaws on the outside. We tend to suffer more from depression, and we'll make a beeline for a shrink's office if we think our brain has gone haywire. Men apparently see asking for help as a sign of weakness, rather like asking for directions.

This doesn't mean that men don't go crazy. They just don't notice it until the guys in the white suits round them up and take them to the Hoo Hoo Hotel, which is 42.5 percent more likely to happen to them than to women.

Those lucky guys don't get bunions very often unless they're given to high-heeled pumps, in which case they deserve what they get. Heaven knows we have paid our killer shoes dues, why shouldn't cross-dressers?

The injustices start in kindergarten, when the boys get more attention from the teacher than the girls. This seems to go on for many years, at least until we develop breasts. But then if the male teacher notices us, he's likely to lose his job.

Show Us the Money

Ah, then we grow up. Perhaps we'll go to college, where 133 females will get BAs for every 100 guys. More women will be in the top of the class, and 61 percent of them will obtain first- or second-class degrees compared with 54 percent of men. And, believe it or not, the IRS says that women will end up bringing home most of the income in U.S. households. Moreover, if you check out the chicks in the high tax brackets, the women have a higher net worth than the men.

It's clear that we know how to make money, but that doesn't begin to measure up to the way we can spend it! After all, we hold the purse strings (read here "pay the bills") in 75 percent of American households. There's no question that women know how to shop better than men, a fact that becomes painfully obvious when you see a man in the produce department of the grocery store, staring helplessly at a stack of cantaloupes. These obviously are not the variety of melons with which he is familiar.

A man will live with his parents longer than a woman will. That's because it takes time for him to find a woman who will do all the crap for him that his mother does. She'll be the one cleaning house (or hiring the cleaning service) and, although the man gets credit for buying the tools, it is she who will end up doing the majority of home improvements. Considering the amount of slave labor expected from a wife, it's amazing that women live on average seven years longer than men.

At least we can take comfort in the knowledge that

one in twelve men is colorblind (only one in two hundred of us is so afflicted). Ah, that would explain speeding through the light as it turns red, for the color-blind man will see it in shades of gray.

A female smiles more than a male, but the man can beat her pits down in the sweating competition. Actually women have more sweat glands than men; we apparently just elect not to put them into service quite so often. Or as my grandmother said, "Girls don't sweat, dear, they glow."

You already know women are more romantic than men, but if you think he makes your heart go pitty pat when he holds you and his just thumps along regularly, don't think it's because he's not excited. It's just that our little hearts beat faster in general, no matter what we're doing. Of course, being behind the wheel of an exotic sports car probably sets his heart pounding like the jack-hammer he sees himself operating in his macho dreams.

Although men and women seem to be equally divided when it comes to being abducted by aliens, men seem overall more inclined to believe in extraterrestrial beings. If the ETs are little *green* men, however, 8.3 percent of human men wouldn't be able to tell, because of that colorblind thing—they'd see them as gray. Could that mean that the people who claim to have been abducted by the gray creatures are all colorblind? We're evenly divided about our four-legged companions. Men are said to prefer dogs, while women love cats. Maybe that's because you can't get a cat to fetch you a beer.

The Barbecue Gene

I've never met a man who couldn't barbecue, or would admit he couldn't. And there's absolutely no way he'll let a woman light the coals.

I think this is similar to the gene that manifests itself early on in teenage boys who feel compelled to jump up and touch the awning as they walk by a store.

Our parenting techniques demonstrate some sort of ancient instinctual perception of what each sex thinks our children need to know in order to survive in the world. A man will put a toy football in the hands of a baby boy before he starts teething; a woman will try to teach him to wave good-bye. Mom will take a child on a walk and point out trees, flowers, and birds. Dad straps the kid in the car seat and takes him to the airport to watch the planes land. And while she will lovingly select only the best organic baby food for her little darling, he can hardly wait to shove a hot dog in the kid's mouth. Weirdest of all, a man who can undress a woman in ten seconds flat, including opening the trickiest of bra clasps, can't seem to manage to get a shirt over a baby's head without nearly suffocating the poor tyke.

Men commit more crimes than women and, once they're caught and convicted, they tend to serve longer prison sentences. Of course, if you could really go to jail for crimes of fashion instead of crimes of passion, there would be a heavy distaff side to the Big House population. And speaking of crime, why is it that women are charged twice as much for dry-cleaning a jacket or getting a simple haircut?

We even handle breaking up differently. Women call and hang up. Guys drive by your house to see if there's someone new parked in your driveway. Men are known to break up via e-mail, but most women prefer a tearful in-person event. Women usually want to remain friends, but guys hardly ever go for it.

Driving the Point Home

Last, but not least, there's the driving issue. Aside from the above-referenced and well-known phobia about directions, men also approach the auto experience as if it were some version of the Pamplona running of the bulls (he and his car being the collective bull) and everybody should just get the hell out of the way. A woman only drives this way if she's late for her massage or manicure appointment. A man cuts into a line of traffic by using his turn signal a couple of times and then just barging in with bravado. A woman delicately waggles her hand out the window in such a manner that it says, "Oh, please, kind sirs, please let me in!" and the sea of cars parts for her. A woman who knows The Ropes knows not to attempt this ploy with other female motorists, for to do so would violate the Sisterhood Road Code. If you've never done it yourself (oh, come on, confess!), it's no urban legend: Women really do use the rearview mirror to apply mascara. But for every time you've seen a woman perform this reckless act of beauty, you've seen ten men picking their noses.

America is a car culture and these days vehicles are equally important to both men and women. They not only provide the necessary transportation, but they can also be a means of self-expression, a statement to the rest of the driving world. A woman of any age who drives a vintage Corvette is intriguing to a man, particularly if she can tell him how she restored it herself. But while a young man in a beautiful old car is charming, a fifty-year-old man who is driving a fully restored Studebaker Golden Hawk is at risk of being perceived as a terminally eccentric car buff who will spend more money on his antique ride than he'll ever spend on a woman.

There's another basic gender-specific disparity in the automotive world. A woman will give an affectionate name like "Sweetiepie" to her car. A man won't bother to name the car since he's already named a personal appendage "Big Fella."

At least one part of the driving experience is divided equally: A man drives *to* the party, but the woman drives home.

Sometimes I wonder if men and women really suit each other. Perhaps they should live next door and just visit now and then.

— KATHARINE HEPBURN

Taken individually these facts may seem trivial, but even the smallest kernel of knowledge is power. Sure, the sexes are vastly different, but we women can use many of these differences to our advantage. We have a whole new set of opportunities in this century, and we have the brains and courage to take advantage of them. We also have more than a few other attributes that can give us an edge in life.

But Wait! There's More!

*The history of all times, and of today especially
teaches that women will be forgotten if they
forget to think about themselves.*

—LOUISE OTTO

s I have diligently tried to suggest throughout this book, this is *not* the beginning of
the end of our lives. I much prefer to believe it is a new
beginning. Let's face it, men in our age group are titans
of industry, still running the company, still considered
to be in their prime. Should women who have spent decades learning, counseling, nurturing, and advising be
expected to retire from life? I think not.

I know whereof I speak. Here I am, at the age of
sixty-two, striking out on a new career path as a writer
and public speaker. And I'm not alone. Many women,
having launched their children into lives of their own,

are setting out to accomplish the things they have dreamed of doing. Women who have become suddenly single after thirty or even forty years of marriage are discovering themselves once again.

We no longer have to wish for things to happen. We can *make* them happen. It's your time, your life. Learn to play the piano. Take a course in fine art history and then travel to Europe to see the real thing. Learn to speak Italian and cook Thai.

It's never too late to become the person you always wanted to be. Get out there, ladies, and conquer the world! After all, now you know The Ropes.

ACKNOWLEDGMENTS

Elinor Klein, Jane Gelfman, Toni Howard, J. B., Kimberly McVay, Dr. Adrienne Stewart, Buzzy, Julie Doughty, and Carole Baron

ABOUT THE AUTHORS

JUDY STEINBERG was married to comedian/director David Steinberg, and has spent the last forty years of her life living and working among some of the great comedy minds of two generations. Judy resides in New York City.

RAECHEL DONAHUE is the author of *The Golden Rules for Modern Romance* and *The Golden Rules for Modern Etiquette*. A popular radio personality, she has a national weekend show broadcast on the Jones Satellite Radio Network and is the nightly host of the syndicated "Moonlight Groove Highway." She lives in Cleveland, Ohio and Venice Beach, California.